101 681 763 0

D1459370

lore Thinking Through Geography

edited by

Adam Nichols
University of Durham

with

David Kinninment
Blyth Community College

series editor

David Leat

The *More Thinking Through Geography* Team

Simon Chandler	King Edward VI School, Morpeth
Nick Chapman	Mornington High School, Wigan *formerly at Kenton School, Newcastle*
David Cookson	Towneley High School, Burnley *formerly at Cramlington High School, Northumberland*
Jackie Downie	Monkwearmouth Comprehensive School, Sunderland
Liz Evans	Haydon Bridge Community High School, Northumberland
Lynda Evans	Gosforth High School, Newcastle
Jen Grundy	Withington Girls' School, Manchester *formerly at Ponteland High School, Northumberland*
David Kinninment	Blyth Community College, Northumberland
David Leat	University of Newcastle upon Tyne
Rachel Lofthouse	University of Newcastle upon Tyne
Julie McGrane	St Thomas More RC Comprehensive School, North Shields
Patty McCoy	St Nicholas Catholic High School, Northwich *formerly at Whitley Bay High School*
Adam Nichols	University of Durham
Amber Riches	The Sanden School, Chelmsford *formerly at Heaton Manor School, Newcastle*

With additional contributions from

Linda Thompson	Sandbach School, Cheshire
Jeremy Krause	Senior Adviser: Geography, Cheshire County Council

© Adam Nichols
2001

ISBN 1 899857 43 5

First published 2001
Reprinted 2001 by
Chris Kington Publishing
27 Rathmore Road
Cambridge CB1 7AB

British Library cataloguing in publication data.

A catalogue record for this book is available from the British Library.

Printed in the United Kingdom by:
Ebenezer Baylis, Worcester.

Designed by:
Character Design, Hereford.

Acknowledgements:
Ralph Hare for *Glossary of Thinking Skills*.
Sarah Maude for photograph on page 46.
The Story of Pedro Morales from *The Inevitable Plan*, Isabel Allende,
1993, HarperCollins

Contents

Chapter 1

More Thinking Through Geography

1 More Thinking Through Geography

Introduction

This book, like its predecessor, *Thinking Through Geography* edited by David Leat (*TTG*) is about raising standards in geography and beyond. The first *TTG* book was written with a bold introduction expressing the desire that geography should become a more challenging subject that focused on helping pupils become better learners. We wanted pupils to be made to think hard, ask questions, be surprised and as a consequence make teachers think hard, ask questions and be surprised.

Many things have happened since that book was published but two are particularly worthy of mention:

1 Many teachers have used the first book, tried the strategies and set in train a process of personal and professional development focusing on pupils' learning. Furthermore many trainee teachers (and not just in geography) use the strategies to invigorate their teaching. This trend is underscored by a Department for Education and Employment (DfEE) research report on *Teaching Thinking* (McGuinness, 1999, p1). The report directed attention to the need to go beyond what is to be learned in a curriculum to 'how children learn and how teachers intervene to achieve this'. The McGuinness report also clarified that curriculum materials are not teacher proof; successful implementation requires an explicit pedagogy and good in-service support in order to create 'thinking classrooms'. Within the *TTG* context this means that *TTG* strategies may yield successful lessons, but teachers need to know how and why they promote thinking. This is why we introduce each strategy with a **Rationale**.

2 The National Curriculum (NC) has been revised again. All subjects at Key Stage 3 are now **required** to include Teaching Thinking (TT), which is specified as: *Information-processing skills; Reasoning skills; Enquiry skills; Creative Thinking skills; and Evaluation skills.* TT is not a whim: it is research evidence based. And it is no longer an optional extra. In some senses this may be regretted, as compulsion is a dubious friend. It is likely to be a jolt to the professional modus operandi of some teachers.

TT has therefore become more mainstream. There is more likelihood of it being supported in schools and LEAs. What becomes more challenging and cutting edge is the need to make it more coherent and the professional development agenda it creates. Just how do you make it work better both with staff and pupils? The first book suggested that there were four Levels of use. These are outlined below. Whilst the first two are still highly appropriate, it is clear that Levels 3 and 4 are becoming a more pressing need.

Levels of use

Level 1. You use Exemplars and their photocopiable materials as they are to create interesting and challenging lessons.

Level 2. All the strategies are flexible and adaptable and can be used across a wide spectrum of ages and ability ranges. To demonstrate this each strategy is exemplified by contexts that range in subject matter and age group. Many of the Exemplars can be used with equal success with Y7 and A Level classes, with only the smallest of changes. We hope that most teachers will be able to use the templates and adapt the strategies for other topics. We know from feedback at INSET courses that many are doing so, sometimes most imaginatively.

Level 3. To the above you start to add **debriefing** through which one gets pupils to talk about their thinking. Thinking and talking about thinking is termed **metacognition**. It is through this process that pupils start to gain an insight into thinking and learning, and build up an explicit understanding of **major concepts in geography** which can be **transferred** to other contexts. We freely acknowledge that debriefing is very hard to do well, especially at first, and can have the effect of making one feel like a novice again. In part this is probably because we ourselves have never really thought about it, never mind developed an appropriate vocabulary with which to discuss it. (see *Appendix*)

Level 4. Beyond Level 3, one is very definitely into the area of school policy relating to curriculum development and staff development. If you want to make TT fully effective it needs to be an approach to teaching found beyond just one department or faculty. There would need to be changes, for example, in policies and practice related to assessment and literacy, and an integrated whole school approach to the curriculum. There are already schools dotted about the country that have taken the plunge. There will be many more.

Raising standards

If *TTG* strategies reinvigorate your teaching, pupils are bound to benefit. But they are no panacea and are intended not to replace but to supplement and complement other forms of good practice. Its forerunners, the CASE (science) and CAME (mathematics) projects benefit from substantially more curriculum time in schools compared with geography and the impacts of their approaches are easier to identify. Research evidence indicates that most pupils perform better with TT in their learning than they might have done without. Recent work by a member of the *TTG* group shows that in the study samples from different schools, greater intensity of TT use produces better results (Chapman, 2001). TT promotes skills that are transferable to other areas of the curriculum. *TTG* is therefore a contributor to pupils' pool of transferable learning skills and a beneficiary of it. The nation-wide interest in the work of the *TTG* group confirms our belief that the strategies help make better geographers by becoming better thinkers and learners.

Amid the plethora of DfEE initiatives to raise standards, TT is one that addresses *how* children think and learn and consciously shares that understanding with them. TT focuses more on what pupils do for themselves than on what teachers do to them. Further more, unlike many of the other initiatives, raising standards through TT is *not* dependent upon large injections of tax payers' money.

Assessment for Learning

Much day to day assessment of pupils' work has been referred to as 'serial summative' in character; that is, it evaluates the quality of the product of one or more pieces of work after the event and informs the pupil of the score. Assessment for Learning requires much more of us than that. In order to support pupils' future endeavours we and they need to understand not just where they go wrong, but why (diagnostic role) and how. We need to help them do it better (formative response).

By focusing on the processes of learning, *TTG* strategies, especially through debriefing, provide evidence and understanding of the ways pupils think and work. In the debriefing discussions, pupils get *immediate* feedback on their reasoning and responses. Consequently, the approaches pupils may adopt to improve their learning are made more explicit. They therefore become critical thinkers, better equipped to 'take responsibility for their own learning' and become 'autonomous learners' - both vacuous terms unless pupils have an inkling of what they can do with responsibility and autonomy!

Where strategies provide particularly useful assessment opportunities, including summatively of KS3 Levels of performance, Exemplars explain how they can be used.

TTG and learning across the curriculum

Geography can make a major contribution to learning across the curriculum. There is plenty of literature and guidance around for subject teachers for promoting citizenship through geography but it is worth highlighting that **developing skills of enquiry and communication** and of **participation and responsible action** are facets of a number of *TTG* strategies, especially those involving decision making.

While it is possible to run some of the strategies with pupils working individually, we are firm advocates of collaborative working and the learning through talking that is involved. This central role of talk and groupwork was discussed in *TTG* (pp160-161). **Working with others** and **communication** are two of the NC's **Key Skills** that form the bedrock of *TTG* strategies. Many of them present pupils with **problem solving** challenges both in specifically geographical contexts and in terms of pupils' approaches to tackling the tasks. Last, but certainly not least, the Key Skill of **improving** (pupils') **own learning and performance** is a basic tenet of *TTG*. Thinking about thinking or **metacognition** was discussed in *TTG* (p159) and the role of debriefing in its development is explored in depth in the **Debriefing** chapter in this book. Improving pupils' own learning is exactly what *TTG* is about.

The NC defines and categorises Thinking Skills in the following way:

By using thinking skills pupils can focus on 'knowing how' as well as 'knowing what' – learning how to learn. The following Thinking Skills complement the Key Skills and are embedded in the National Curriculum.

Information–processing skills

These enable pupils to locate and collect relevant information, to sort, classify, sequence, compare and contrast, and to analyse part/whole relationships.

Reasoning skills

These enable pupils to give reasons for opinions and actions, to draw inferences and make deductions, to use precise language to explain what they think, and to make judgements and decisions informed by reasons or evidence.

Enquiry skills

These enable pupils to ask relevant questions, to pose and define problems, to plan what to do and how to research, to predict outcomes and anticipate consequences, and to test conclusions and improve ideas.

Creative Thinking skills

These enable pupils to generate and extend ideas to suggest hypotheses, to apply imagination, and to look for alternative imaginative outcomes.

Evaluation skills

These enable pupils to evaluate information, to judge the value of what they read, hear and do, to develop criteria for judging the value of their own and others' work or ideas, and to have confidence in their judgements.

(DfEE, 1999, pp 23-4)

TTG strategies are rich in **Thinking Skills**. Where the Exemplars here in More Thinking Through Geography strongly employ and develop particular kinds, they are identified in The Exemplars (see pp6–7). The strategies in TTG are equally rich and teachers who are familiar with them would readily identify which of the thinking skills above are developed through them. There are numerous examples of TTG activities incorporated into the QCA A Geography Scheme of Work for KS3 (QCA, 2000) and some teachers who are unfamiliar with TTG strategies have been a little baffled to know what they are and how to operationalise them. In this sense, Thinking Through Geography and More Thinking Through Geography are valuable companions to many of the units in the scheme of work.

Using the Exemplars

We use the term **Exemplar** in its true meaning of something serving as a model. TTG strategies are intended to be flexible in their application. Each one has been tried and tested by members of the Newcastle-based TTG group in many subject contexts across the age and ability ranges and in a wide variety of schools from leafy suburbs to the inner city.

There are eight strategies in this book. For those readers who have worked with TTG it might be useful to think of these in addition to the eight strategies introduced in TTG. It is emphasised however that More Thinking Through Geography stands on its own as a fully self-contained teacher resource.

In common with TTG through which the first eight strategies were introduced, each strategy has a **Rationale**. The strategy is explained in terms of its value to pupils' learning and some of the ways in which it helps to overcome obstacles to learning that pupils frequently face. Aspects of the enthusiasm that the teacher has for the strategy often come through in this section. The theoretical basis which underpins each strategy has been consciously avoided in the text to spare the reader, but may be explored through the references in the marginal notes and bibliography.

Each Exemplar is provided with the **Context** within which it was used which helps the reader to make sense of the accounts of the lessons. However, the use of Exemplars is not tied to these particular circumstances, though the activation of prior knowledge and experience is important in some instances.

Preparation, as with any lesson, is crucial for the success of a strategy, particularly until the teacher has really got the hang of it. These are the antithesis of double-page-spread and worksheet lessons and they are not easy to do off the cuff but *they are worth doing*. They require pupils' active participation in the learning process, so issues of clarity of instructions, management of pupils, resources, time and how to launch and close must all be considered.

Each Exemplar describes the various ways in which the teacher launched the activity. **Launching** prepares the ground perhaps by drawing on pupils' existing knowledge and interests, tapping their ideas, employing an analogy and capturing their interests. As pupils become increasingly familiar and experienced with the strategies, less of this tends to be needed. **Instructions**, though, will always need to be clear. Those given in each Exemplar are the principle directions for the activity to run. There were many more, often of a transactional or managerial nature, that have not been included.

In addition to the instructions, the teacher is involved in **managing the activity** with a particular view to supporting the learning process. Pupils who are engaged in meaningful and 'effortful' activities tend to require less intervention from the teacher. They will get stuck and frustrated at times and the teacher must keep a weather-eye open for those needing support to move them on by helping them to negotiate the challenge rather than remove it. As they make progress, so the scaffolding provided by the teacher can be reduced. It is the pupils who do most of the talking too, and you cannot expect to run these strategies in silence.

Each strategy describes the **debriefing** process that follows the activity. Its function is to discuss and make explicit the thinking processes and strategies employed by pupils and to encourage transfer of the thinking to other contexts. This is the real pay-off. The emphasis in the debriefing phase varies in relation to the stage each class is at in the development of its thinking about thinking and skill level at each strategy. Debriefing is fully discussed in Chapter 12.

Ideas for ways to **follow-up** the activities are provided which build upon the learning outcomes of the lesson. Many have a reflective or a speculative dimension that involves turning thinking into the written word. Many pupils as well as teachers gain a sense of security from producing tangible evidence of their learning, but written work is only one of many alternatives. Suggestions for developing or **adapting the strategy** are then appended together with attention being drawn to the potential for associating them with other *TTG* activities.

Lastly there are some **afterthoughts** that are the teachers' reflections on pitfalls, successes and approaches to improving the way the strategy was used. They are evidence of the learning cycle that practising TT geographers generally regard as part of their professional development.

There is variety of style and emphasis too. Some are well run-in strategies, others are still evolving and the descriptions reflect some of the unpredictability of the latter, while ideas for adaptation and extension are well developed in the former. Things do go wrong. We have not written up the fiascos, but they happen. (Safe 'double page spread' lessons can fail too in their own way.) There is an element of risk in employing *TTG* strategies, the hallmarks of which are challenge, active participation, variety, collaboration, differentiation and, of course, *enjoyment*. Furthermore, they address the range of preferred learning styles of our pupils, which is why some strategies work superbly with mixed ability classes. We have used the terms 'pupil' and 'student' interchangeably, reflecting the particular preferences of the contributing teachers.

The Exemplars are not sacred cows. Chop, change, cut, stick, re-locate, re-word to your heart's content, but try not to lose sight of the *thinking* objectives. Rather depressingly, we have come across Exemplars from *TTG* that have been gutted of TT and converted into comprehension exercises. This illustrates the need for professional development as no curriculum materials are teacher-proof.

On the other side of the coin, improvements, improvisations and new applications are great to see. That is exactly what we hoped would happen. There are many areas of the geography curriculum that our Exemplars have not touched yet. Go for it!

The Exemplars

Strategy (Topic & Year)	Big Concepts	NC Thinking Skills	Other Learning Outcomes
Most Likely To.... Exemplar 1: Tourism in the Rainforests Y9	Classification, location	IP, R, CT, Ev.	Speculating, comparing, values, citizenship
Most Likely To.... Exemplar 2: Farming in the UK Y10	Classification, location	IP, R, CT, Ev.	Speculating, comparing, explaining, visual literacy
Maps From Memory Exemplar 1: Urban Transport in Newcastle-upon-Tyne Y10/11	Systems, location	IP, Ev	Visual literacy, sketching, memorising
Maps From Memory Exemplar 2: The British Isles using KS3 Map D Y7/8/9	Systems, location	IP, Ev	Visual literacy, sketching, memorising
Maps From Memory Exemplar 3: Destructive Plate Margins Y8/9	Systems, location	IP, Ev	Visual literacy, sketching, memorising
Making Animals Exemplar 1: Making Animals & Plants Y7–12	Cause & effect, systems	IP, R, En, CT, Ev	Application, using pupils' knowledge, explaining
Making Animals Exemplar 2: Migration - Packing for a Journey Y8/9	Cause & effect, planning, decision making	IP, R, En, CT, Ev	Application, using pupils' knowledge, reading, explaining
Making Animals Exemplar 3: Improving a Shanty Town Y10/11 Exemplar 4: Improving a Rural Village Y7–9	Cause & effect, planning, decision making, development	IP, R, En, CT, Ev	Application, using pupils' knowledge, explaining
Five Ws Exemplar 1: The San Francisco Earthquake 1989 Y9	Cause & effect, planning, decision making	IP, R, En, Ev	Developing vocabulary, questioning, researching, reading, drafting, extended writing
Five Ws Exemplar 1: Farming in Upland Areas Y10/11	Cause & effect, planning, decision making	IP, R, En, Ev	Developing vocabulary, questioning, researching, drafting, extended writing, visual literacy
Five Ws Exemplar 1: Natural Environments Y9	Cause & effect	IP, R, En, Ev	Developing vocabulary, drafting, teamwork, peer assessment
Taboo Exemplar 1: The Water Cycle Y8	Systems	R, CT, Ev	Drafting, developing vocabulary, explaining, describing
Taboo Exemplar 2: Settlement Y10/11	Location	R, CT, Ev	Drafting, developing vocabulary, explaining, describing

Strategy (Topic & Year)	Big Concepts	NC Thinking Skills	Other Learning Outcomes
Layered Decision Making Exemplar 1: Migration - The Stuarts Move House Y7–10	Cause & effect, planning, decision making, classification	IP, R, En, CT, Ev	Empathy, active listening, conflict resolution
Layered Decision Making Exemplar 2: Dam the Consequences Y9–12	Cause & effect, planning, decision making, development, classification	IP, R, En, CT, Ev	Empathy, active listening, conflict resolution
Layered Decision Making Exemplar 3: A New Stadium for Middleton United? Y9–12	Cause & effect, planning, decision making, development, classification	IP, R, En, CT, Ev	Empathy, active listening, conflict resolution, ICT
Concept Maps Exemplar 1: Comparing Earthquakes Y8/9	Classification, cause & effect, inequality	IP, R	Extended writing, explaining
Concept Maps Exemplar 2: The Decline of Deep Mining Y10/11	Classification, cause & effect	IP, R	Extended writing, explaining, economic understanding
Concept Maps Exemplar 3: The Three Gorges Dam Y12/13	Classification, cause & effect, systems, development	IP, R	Explaining, extended writing, reading, citizenship
Predicting with Video Exemplar 1: Migration in North East Brazil Y9	Cause & effect	IP, R, En, CT, Ev	Extended writing, empathy, moral dilemmas, visual literacy, active listening, citizenship
Predicting with Video Exemplar 2: Conflict & Change in Urban Areas Y12	Cause & effect, planning, inequality, decision making.	IP, R, En, CT, Ev	Speculating, comparing, explaining, political process, visual literacy, active listening, citizenship
Predicting with Video Exemplar 3: Coastal Processes Y10/11	Systems, cause & effect	IP, R, En, CT, Ev	Speculating, explaining, debating, visual literacy, active listening

Big Concepts elaborated through debriefing.

Other important learning outcomes relating to skill areas, types of literacy, citizenship, etc. Collaboration is an integral part of all these strategies.

NC Thinking Skills:

IP = Information Processing;

R = Reasoning;

En = Enquiry;

CT = Creative Thinking;

Ev = Evaluation.

All of the strategies involve group work and debriefing and therefore promote NC Key Skills of Communication, Working with Others, and Improving own Learning and Performance. Most deal with Problem Solving to a greater or lesser degree. Only one (A New Stadium for Middleton United?) specifies using ICT though other opportunities are plentiful.

More Thinking Through Geography

Chapter 2

Most Likely To....

2 Most Likely To....

Rationale

Most Likely To.... is very straightforward to devise and implement and it can be easily incorporated into your schemes of work to great effect and minimal effort - a real bonus! It involves presenting students with a list of options and requires them to identify which they think are most likely to be representative of or to characterise a given situation, activity or location.

If one of geography's functions is to identify and understand patterns and processes at work in the physical and human environments then it is also about making generalisations which we might also call mental models. These provide the geographer with frameworks with which to examine and interpret new situations. Many students need to be encouraged to transfer their learning from one context to another. Most Likely To.... helps students to build, test and modify their understanding of generalisations.

Identifying the characteristics of places, activities and people is an everyday activity in life and one we ask geography students to do a lot. Most Likely To.... helps students to do this better. Readers may have encountered the strategy in *Exemplar 2* of **Reading Photographs** in *TTG* in the context of models of urban land use and you may hear echoes of **Odd One Out** which builds a similar skill base. As with a number of *TTG* strategies, it hinges on the ability to sort, classify and link information.

Most Likely To.... has a number of strengths in contributing to students' learning:

- experience indicates that it helps improve students' ability to process information and to attach meaning;
- students develop their understanding of **characteristics**;
- the strategy further develops **classifying** skills;
- it helps students to test their understanding of **generalisations** and to generate their own;
- through discussion, students clarify their understanding of and explore the limitations of **generalisations**: (Likelihood is another word for probability which pupils understand well from KS3 maths!)
- it involves testing **hypotheses**;
- it is a form of enquiry that causes pupils to ask geographical questions;
- some statements are ambiguous and therefore very thought provoking;
- it enhances students' understanding and memory of geographical **vocabulary**;
- students **visualise** context and content as they talk and work through the task which aids long term retention of ideas and information.

To get the most out of the activity, Most Likely To.... needs to be thoroughly debriefed. The words in bold above are all key vocabulary that could be explored not so much for the benefit of the geographical content but for developing awareness and understanding of the processes involved in the activity. (see *Appendix*) This is addressed at the end of each Exemplar.

In its simplest form, it should more properly be called 'More likely to...' because only two alternatives are provided (*Exemplar 1*). The strategy can become increasingly challenging as the number of alternatives is raised.

There are some risks inherent in this strategy and before rushing headlong into it you should refer to the *Health Warning* in the **afterthoughts** to *Exemplar 1*.

Most Likely To.... encourages pupils to think more critically about stereotypes in other contexts.

Collectively these are forms of critical thinking. They relate strongly to the five NC Thinking Skills.

This is **metacognition** or thinking about thinking.

Tourism in the Rainforests

Context

This large, lively and enthusiastic mixed ability Y9 class had a track record of willingness to try new activities. This 50 minute lesson came near the end of a unit of work on the rainforests during which we had studied location, the ecosystem including wildlife, climate, indigenous people, deforestation and addressed some conservation issues. They had some experience of *TTG* activities and were fairly comfortable with discussing what they had learnt from the activity and how they had tackled it. On this occasion, **Most Likely To....** was a stepping stone and preparation task for an end of unit assessment task on ecotourism as a management strategy for sustainable development in the rainforests. They had some knowledge of large-scale commercial tourism from a previous unit on the Mediterranean.

Preparation

I usually have pupils working in pairs for this activity but because follow-up work would involve homework each pupil needed a copy of *Resource 1* and a sheet of file paper on which to make notes of their choices and reasoning. You or your pupils will need to draw a matrix with the two types of tourism on one axis and numbered choices on the other.

Decide how long you want to spend on this activity. It is very elastic. While the factual characteristics can be dispensed with quickly, those with ambiguity can grow into full-scale debates. I feel that the real learning takes place through the discussion. The limits of meaning and understanding are explored through it, so after between 5 and 10 minutes **launching**, I planned for the next 20 minutes to be working in pairs and the remaining 20 minutes discussing their decisions and in **debriefing**.

Safe in the knowledge that you will have taken a look at the **afterthoughts** to this strategy, now is the time for some forethought. As a result of this activity (or indeed, previous lessons) might pupils conclude: that large-scale commercial tourism is automatically evil? that ecotourism isn't itself commercial? that all indigenous people want this kind of development? that indigenous people are a live part of the 'theme park' like a trip to Beamish Museum? There are other possibilities. You need to be aware of these so that you can examine these conceptions and assumptions later.

Launching

The pupils are football-mad, yes, even many of the girls, so I led off by asking who were Newcastle United supporters. A sea of hands went up accompanied by some light-hearted banter with the 'traitors' who had not put theirs up. I asked these if they supported another team. A couple dared admit to following Manchester United and another pair had no interest in the game. I then said, 'Suppose I asked the same question in a Sunderland, or a Leicester school. What response might I expect?' After the inevitable comment about being stupid to support either local team, the class quickly came round to the idea that like themselves, they were *most likely to* support their local team but *not necessarily*. They may have other reasons for supporting a different one such as when local 'boy' Shearer played for Blackburn, or if they lived somewhere else previously.

> This introduction helps motivate pupils and put the learning in a wider relevant context.

I then asked them for some characteristics of Newcastle United. Answers ranged from the factual: home ground St. James' Park; managed by Bobby Robson; magpie mascot - to the subjective (and even laughable!): best supporters in the land; premiership champions - next year, (always). I invited the infidels for their views on these comments. They were not impressed.

They were a bit puzzled by all this so I told them that they would be putting these ideas to use with the likely characteristics of two types of tourism in the rainforest. We quickly brainstormed what we could remember about (most!) tourism on the Mediterranean and how ecotourism is different.

I distributed the statement sheet (*Resource 1*) and asked if they wanted anything clarifying: '*What's the local team called, Miss?*' Some questions you just can't answer.

Instructions

1 Get pupils into pairs. I usually let them work with the person sitting next to them.

2 Explain that the jumbled up statements on the sheet (*Resource 1*) could be characteristics of two kinds of tourism that could be developed in the rainforests. They might apply to ecotourism, mass commercial tourism or perhaps both. The task is to sort them into two groups according to which they think *most likely to* be characteristics of the two types of tourism. They can tackle the statements in any order.

3 Ask them to decide as they go along which person would explain their decision if asked to do so at the end of the activity and to try and share them fairly. (This ploy encourages them to discuss rather than guess!)

4 If you opt for the follow-up activity, tell them that they will need to understand the characteristics of each of these two types of tourism because they will be preparing a report on the appropriateness of different types of tourism in the rainforests.

5 Tell them to make notes of their decisions and reasoning.

Managing the activity

Pupils record their **Most Likely To....** decisions and reasoning in the matrix as described earlier. Ticks can be put in the appropriate column. To avoid breaking and slowing the flow of the lesson, do not ask pupils to write the statements out. They already have a copy! Sometimes the discussion is a satisfactory end in itself and recording may be dispensed with altogether. It is up to you.

This is an activity that is really easy to manage. It suits almost all arrangements of furniture and involves so few resources. You can decide whether or not to let pupils consult their exercise book, textbooks or atlases to help them 'research' their decisions. After all it isn't an exam. You must judge if the knowledge base of the class is adequate for the activity not to become a wild guessing game. It is pretty pointless if it does.

Start the groups off at different points in the list of characteristics so all of them get considered by someone. You have to keep an ear out for those discussions that turn into off-task chat but this can usually be controlled by 'physical proximity', asking them to justify one of their decisions, and by pacing. Urge them on if it looks like some are flagging. Some pairs are bound to finish before others (depending on motivation, ability and depth of discussion). First check that the quick ones have done a thorough job then set them an additional open ended task of devising some extra statements of their own that will allow them to show off their extra knowledge!

Don't let the activity go on too long or they can start getting bored. I stopped when the majority seemed to have finished. Those who hadn't, benefitted from the following open forum anyway.

Debriefing

This was a major part of the lesson. I asked if they had found the activity challenging. One boy said the statement about tourists offending local people seemed obvious at first: that the commercial tourists were less aware of or interested in local people's way of lives and weren't warned of what was acceptable or not, so they'd be *more likely to* offend them. I encouraged him to go on. Then they thought of package holidays in the sun that they had had when they'd hardly met any local people anyway, so maybe, since they keep separate, the local people wouldn't be upset by their presence or behaviour. Perhaps, they thought, that with ecotourists spending most of their time in the company of local people there might be more opportunity to give offence. '*And, I wouldn't want a bunch of foreigners wandering round my estate taking pictures of me, thank you very much.*' I thought this was terrific reasoning, as did the rest of the class so I was more than happy with this extended contribution.

This sparked off other debates (treading a fine line between debate and argument) about which kind of holiday would be the more expensive. One girl said she'd thought ecotours because unspoiled places are difficult to get to. Others thought it was ridiculous to imagine that sleeping in wooden huts would cost as much as a posh hotel. Then another girl chipped in perceptively '*Yes, but when something's unusual and not many people do it or have something, things are more expensive, like, if you wanted a car that nobody else had, it would probably be dead expensive.*'

Economic processes, accessibility, human behaviour, values and attitudes and transfer of ideas between contexts: an impressive cocktail of ideas were being interlinked in these two exchanges alone. Indeed, much of the debriefing discussion was centred on these two statements.

So, which kind of tourism would they go for? Ecotours meant fewer trees being felled, but there was some concern that the local population wouldn't remain unaffected by even this type of tourism. Tourists might 'give them ideas' with their smart clothing, cameras. They might start to want things they can't have. The class couldn't decide which kind of tourism would leave local people financially better off. A common phrase in discussions like these is 'it depends', which, of course, it does!

Finally, I was running out of time so concluded by asking how they thought the activity might have helped them understand ecotourism. A couple of people said they felt they could imagine more easily what it might be like to go on an ecotour. Someone wondered if you could have ecotourism anywhere and we left the lesson thinking about that.

> High level thinking is characterised by pupils appreciating that more than one answer or solution is possible.

Follow-up

A second lesson and homework was allocated to individually written reports on the advantages and disadvantages of ecotourism over mass commercial tourism in the rainforest environment. I encouraged them to include as many of the ideas from the statements list and their notes. Because they were not in any order, sorting the ideas out into some sort of order would be important. I had available two differentiated versions of a writing frame for those that floundered at this stage. A few pupils needed this kind of support.

Assessment

I applied NC Level descriptions in assessing the completed reports as the finished work was destined for their KS3 portfolios of work. Some had found it hard and had not made as much use of the **Most Likely To....** statements as I hoped. Others incorporated ideas from the open discussion phase to enrich their arguments. The very best showed that they appreciated that there were often conditions under which something could be either a benefit or a disadvantage.

> This illustrates the process of general dialogue becoming internalised and later used in personal writing.

The task was very open ended and I did not specify a particular written style or mode of presentation, so the report task was inherently differentiated. It also allowed them to draw upon personal experiences of holidays, though for some these were limited to the UK. All in all, the resulting work was impressive.

The following characteristics of work were used to assign Levels. The range of Levels made accessible by this activity demonstrates its power to differentiate.

NC Level	Description of levels of response
3	Simple comparisons of the two kinds of tourism.
4	More detailed description and comparisons and some explanation of their impacts on the rainforest environment.
5	Clear explanations of ecotourism and commercial tourism, their environmental impacts and understanding of ecotourism as an approach to sustainable development of the rainforest.
6	Description and explanation of ecotourism as a means of environmental protection and sustainable development including appreciation of the positive and negative impacts on local communities.
7	Explanation of the advantages and disadvantages of the types of tourism in terms of environmental, social and economic impact and appreciation of potential of ecotourism as a form of sustainable development.
8	A balanced evaluation of the two kinds of tourism, an appreciation of the vulnerability of the rainforest environment and its inhabitants and an understanding of how ecotourism can be an approach to managing development in a sustainable way.

Afterthoughts

Don't ignore this bit. There is a general *Health Warning* that comes with this strategy: this is the danger of engendering or reinforcing stereotypes and prejudices that students may have, not only about people and environments of which they have no personal experience but also those that they do. Some of the attitudes harboured by students (and perhaps teachers too) that they bring to the activity may not be supported by facts or are incongruent with the big picture. In this Exemplar, pupils sometimes have stereotypical images of and attitudes to tour companies, tourists and indigenous peoples. In *Exemplar 3* consider the characteristics of different zones of a city and a question such as 'in which zone is car theft most likely to happen?' Students' responses might be based upon where they believe most thieves to live. However, the main gain comes from group discussion and from debriefing which may explore other associated factors such as where are cars more likely to be garaged and where the most valuable or easiest cars to steal might be found.

Addressing stereotypes harnesses Reasoning skills, Enquiry skills and Evaluation skills NCTS.

The strategy can in fact be used to *challenge* stereotypes by asking such questions as 'is that the *only* circumstance where x occurs...?' in the debriefing, if pupils themselves have not been asking it. The absence of laws in geography (well, *I* can't think of any) is indicative that patterns and generalisations are not watertight. This is essential understanding if pupils are to be able to relate *their* geographies to the key ideas we are trying to teach. Take, for instance, the ideas associated with the growth of 'out of town' hypermarkets. Individual pupils from their own domestic circumstances may know that car owners are not obliged to shop there, nor is a car a requirement to do so (Some people live nearby and some minibuses bring the elderly!). From KS3 onwards, pupils have a good grasp of probability and possibility acquired from life if not from maths. We are doing pupils and the subject a disservice if we present geography as a set of unquestionable truths.

Ecotourism or Mass Commercial Tourism?

Most likely to....

1	enable profits from tourism to reach local people	**13**	provide all the services and facilities that tourists might want
2	employ local people	**14**	develop a sense of trust and friendship between the tourists
3	benefit large tour companies	**15**	develop a sense of trust and friendship between tourists and local people
4	bring crime to the rainforests	**16**	strengthen the communities of the rainforest
5	be a community-led programme	**17**	have a welcome meeting from the tour representative
6	be intrusive to local people	**18**	be very expensive
7	involve small numbers of tourists	**19**	allow tourists to 'observe' local people in their native habitat
8	disturb the wildlife of the rainforest	**20**	provide only basic facilities
9	involve wild late night parties	**21**	result in tourists offending local people
10	endanger the survival of rainforest plant and animal species	**22**	teach people traditional crafts and life skills of the forest
11	encourage local people to move to the cities	**23**	involve lots of sunbathing
12	be educational for the tourists	**24**	eat the local food and drink the local drink
		25	cause waste and pollution

Farming in the UK

Context

I have used this as part of a 50 minute lesson with three different Y10 classes over three consecutive years about three weeks into the unit, so it is well run-in! It slots into a unit on agriculture in SEG syllabus A. Though our groups are all mixed ability, the make-up and size does vary. This Exemplar describes how it worked with one of the smaller groups whose general ability was towards the lower end of the spectrum. They do have motivational problems, find concentration and co-operation difficult and they sometimes can't see the point of what they are doing. I have tried a number of thinking skills activities with them before but poor discussion skills, especially listening, had left me disappointed and discouraged, though I know Rome wasn't built in a day! However, not being one to be beaten I was determined to continue to work at improving these vital skills. This was a good proving ground for a *TTG* strategy!

The class had previously looked at factors influencing farming types in the UK using standard textbooks and various video clips. They had some understanding of the inputs, processes and outputs of arable farming in the Cambridgeshire fens and hill farming in the Lake District.

Preparation

Because of the ability level, this Exemplar has fewer ambiguous and more readily recognisable statements than the others do. However it is very easy for you to raise the level of challenge by adding to the list and removing some others.

As with *Exemplar 1*, this was a paired activity but in the event of disaster, I prepared enough copies of *Resource 2* for them to work independently if required. (ie, just in case the lesson disintegrated) Each student drew their own decision recording matrix as outlined in *Exemplar 1*.

Launching

'How many of you watched 'Eastenders' last night?' Most put up their hands. *'Well, I didn't, so can someone tell me what happened, please?'* One of the girls began an extraordinarily comprehensive account of the goings on in Albert Square, helped along by comments tossed in by other pupils. *'If only you could remember as much about your last geography lesson!'*, I said. That raised a few laughs and one or two comments I won't bother to repeat here.

I then made reference to the video clips they had watched about farming and asked them what they could remember about the two farms they had seen. Contrary to my expectations, they could describe a lot: where they were; what they were like; what they grew; and so on.

I said that I was going to test their memories of the two farms studied in the last lesson (groans) but that they could do it in pairs (sighs of relief). I said that they would need to remember something about the characteristics of the farming types so what were 'characteristics'? This resulted in a few blank faces until I illustrated what I meant by characteristics: 'Paul is male with fair hair and usually late. Sarah is female, dark-haired, and punctual. These are some of the characteristics of Paul and Sarah.' From this episode, I'm pretty sure they got the idea that they understood that characteristics are what make someone recognisable, distinct and even unique.

Instructions

These were as for *Exemplar 1*. They were told that they could do this alone, but if they wanted they could work with their partner. They chose to work with a partner. This was an attempt to give them a sense of responsibility for how the lesson ran.

I told them to enter the names of the two types of farms at the top of the choice columns on the recording sheet. I then said that the statements on the sheet were characteristics that apply to one of the farms they had already seen. Their job was to decide which statements were **Most Likely To....** fit with each farm type and showing their choice with a tick and a reason for choosing it. I said that some could (within the students' understanding) apply to both farms, in which case they could tick both columns. I reminded them that most of the activity on a hill

> Remember that these are Exemplars to be adapted and developed.

> The constructivist notion that new learning is based upon existing knowledge and understanding is borne out here.

> We often underestimate the power and value of visual memory. This is tapped in **Maps From Memory** and **Predicting with Video.**

> These are NCTS Information Processing skills

More Thinking Through Geography

farm actually takes place in the valleys and to think more about that than the hilltops. I gave them a quarter of an hour for this activity.

Managing the activity

There are members of this class who can fly off the handle or enjoy provoking others, so I spread the pairs around the room. I 'sold' this to them by suggesting that if they were near other pairs, they could be overheard. Unfortunately this seemed to inhibit discussion a bit so I opened the window to bring in a bit of traffic noise and that helped to 'hide' the exposure of discussion.

Pace is important with this group so I kept each section brief and defined by a time limit. I gave them 15 minutes for the activity though they took a little longer. This seemed to keep them more focused than usual. One pair, though, was squabbling so they accepted my 'suggestion' that they work individually. Interestingly though, once they saw how the others were discussing and getting on, they too started to ask each other questions. I paid regular visits to encourage them to talk through to me what they understood by some of the statements such as 'short growing season'. They knew that it was the time of year when crops grew but needed some support to appreciate that its length was governed by temperatures: how early in the year spring arrived and how late winter started. It is quite a sophisticated concept when you think about it.

In retrospect, I wished I had taken advantage of the sometimes extensive personal experience of many of the students, townies though they are, of local farms whether through horse riding, mountain biking or other activities. To connect with and to recognise the value of their own knowledge I could have added an extra column to the recording sheet for them to identify characteristics that are in common with the study farms and the one they know well. Pupils could then generate some **Most Likely To....** statements that would apply to the farm they know.

Debriefing

My previous attempts at debriefing have not been too successful with students either reluctant to share ideas or resorting to silly comments but I wanted to try again. I had made a mental note of some of the discussion I had over-heard while circulating and asked the pairs to remember what they had said with words along the line of *'That's good thinking. I'll ask you to repeat that when we discuss the activity later. Make a note of it'*. I was hoping that by being warned in advance they might feel more confident of the value of their contribution and help kick start the discussion.

I wanted this to be a positive experience so used the opportunity for plenty of praise. I knew that all pairs had worked their way through the whole list of characteristics more or less thoughtfully so I could congratulated them for that. No one complained that it was too hard. I asked some of them for their decisions about a few of the more straightforward statements such as 'be in a lowland area' in order to be able to spread more praise. Then I had an unplanned brainwave: Why not try a **Mind Movie**?

I told them to shut their eyes and imagine the scene I was going to describe to them. From their glances they clearly thought I'd lost the plot, but they all obliged. I began to describe a walk through a farm by including some of the characteristics of the Cambridgeshire farm from their list but without naming it. I asked them to open their eyes and put their hands up if they could identify the farm. Only 3 or 4 didn't. I chose one of the girls (who gave the right answer) to explain. She said she could see big, flat fields stretched way out ahead with crops spread all over it. Others said they could see the farm buildings in some detail too and some features that were not specified in the statement list. Most of them seemed to have a good visual image of this farm, much of which probably matched what they had seen on the video the previous week but I didn't have time to unpick this nor whether or not they held strong mental images of a hill farm too.

Most of the class was able to contribute to this phase of the lesson so I lavished them with more praise before giving them the **follow-up** task. They (and I) were in much better spirits than usual!

Smith (1998) has some good ideas on creating productive learning environments.

This is progress in the Key Skill of Working with Others.

Groups getting stuck are being scaffolded here.

This is an excellent way to support one's debriefing.

See *TTG* p39

Follow-up

This was to be a straightforward written comparison of farming in Cambridgeshire and the Lake District in which they would identify any similarities they could find as well as contrasts. This occupied the last 10 minutes of the lessons and was finished for homework. *Resource Sheet 2* was available to help them and they had to include as many characteristics as possible. In the nick of time, I decided to make more use of their visual memories by asking them to draw a picture of the two farms as they could see them with their eyes shut and to label them. Not everyone felt themselves to be good enough artists for this but I said I wanted a sketch, not an artwork and they seemed to be happier with that.

When the homework was handed in next lesson, I was pleased that some of the drawings had turned out very well indeed with colour, farm vehicles and so on. There was plenty of detailed but separate description of the two farms. The idea of *comparison* was not clearly understood and I made a mental note to return to this skill area again.

This connects with Gardner's notion of 'multiple intelligences'. Pupils know and can do more than they reveal or we discover but we have to try to find ways to help them access it.

A formative response in future planning of a key geographical skill that is often required but not often explicitly taught.

Cambridgeshire Fens or the Lake District?

Resource 2

Which farms are most likely to....

1	cover large areas of countryside	**16**	have soils which are low in nutrients
2	have a short growing season	**17**	have a problem with foxes
3	use natural stone for their buildings	**18**	use high technology
4	have enormous sheds for machinery	**19**	welcome campers
5	have flat land	**20**	welcome genetic modification
6	grow fodder crops to feed their **own** livestock	**21**	pollute local streams
7	have high rainfall figures	**22**	have few workers
8	use large quantities of fertilizers and pesticides	**23**	make big profits some years
9	take their own products to market	**24**	use a muck spreader
10	have dykes and drains to control water levels	**25**	have a wide choice of what can be produced
11	make hay from grass	**26**	have an interrupted night's sleep in spring
12	depend upon government subsidies	**27**	be caught out by frost in late spring
13	work through the night in late summer	**28**	take a sunshine holiday in the winter
14	pay vet's fees	**29**	go to work on a quad bike some days
15	have rain all year round	**30**	be owned by a food processing company

Chapter 3

Maps From Memory

3 Maps From Memory

Rationale

One of the attractions of geography for many learners is its use of visual material. However, visual skills vary from person to person and understanding and interpretation (decoding the message) of maps and diagrams is a major obstacle for some children. If the spatial dimension is central to our discipline, we must consciously help pupils to appreciate how maps and diagrams convey particular information.

We have met the pupil who shades in the landmasses and who clearly lacks understanding of graphical representation. For some pupils, maps are aesthetic patterns not necessarily understood. NC geography at KS3 distinguishes between developing the skills to *use* maps (2c) and the ability to *construct* them independently (2e). We often require pupils to draw sketch maps and diagrams though we actually want them to make *copies* of them from a textbook, the board or OHT. If so, we may be guilty of missing the target (2e) altogether. Even so, the purpose is generally to encode and record information and concepts that have been addressed in a lesson. They are shorthand for the meaning we want pupils to internalise. In other words, they have a cognitive rather than illustrative or decorative function.

The process of making use of maps and diagrams involves three steps. Firstly, identifying the component parts by detecting one kind of symbolic representation from another. The second is recognition of what the symbols represent and the third step is interpretation of what the spatial distributions of the symbols mean (eg, that a trunk road links place x to place y along a valley). **Maps From Memory** stimulates these processes.

Clearly, recalling and understanding are not the same thing, but remembering maps and diagrams and being able to draw them from memory can be a key to unlocking the understanding associated with them. We have drawn attention to the role of visual memory in the **Mind Movies** strategy (*TTG*). We suggested there that explicitly encouraging the use of the visual memory is empowering for less able pupils whose literacy levels are low. This is also a strength of the **Reading Photographs** strategy (*TTG*) which causes pupils to interrogate images for meaning. **Maps From Memory** is similarly a useful vehicle for differentiation. It involves memorising what is seen as well as what is understood and is an activity that is accessible to the full ability range.

For such an important skill, there are plenty of opportunities to interpret but surprisingly few to draw maps from memory in GCSE examinations, although coursework assignments would be incomplete without them. Some GCSE syllabuses only mention sketch map and diagram drawing in that particular context. Some A Level exam rubrics state that credit will be given for drawing sketch maps and diagrams, but examiners report annually that candidates do not do so, even in support of case studies. Examiners also comment that pupils often don't make full use of graphical data provided in exam questions. This strategy encourages them to look at it more carefully.

Maps From Memory is great fun. It has the advantage over 'Kim's Game' in that what is to be remembered is meaningfully related. We have used it with all year groups and at the starts, middles and ends of topics. It is a lively way of encouraging pupils to look carefully at the component parts of maps and diagrams and to devise strategies to help commit them to memory. In the process, they explore the meaning of the maps and diagrams and call up and make connections with knowledge they already have about the subject matter. Furthermore, teamwork and communication skills are encouraged in a good-humoured, competitive way.

Too many pupils turn their backs on geography at the end of KS3 in the belief that they 'can't do' or 'don't understand' maps. One 'refusnik' told me that she thought maps to geography were like trigonometry was to her mathematics. She could go through the motions without understanding what they were about. In a competitive curriculum we need to address this shortcoming. We think that **Maps From Memory** is a strategy that has value in all key stages and post-16. It is a significant advance on telling pupils to 'Go home and learn that. It might come up in the exam!' without showing them how.

Gardner (1983) calls this ability to graphically represent and interpret visual and spatial ideas 'spatial intelligence'. This strategy supports pupils' development of visual literacy.

Sometimes pupils are asked to engage in step 3 before having a grasp of the previous 2! They often confuse boundaries, coastlines and rivers.

These are both NC Key Skills.

Competition has been identified as a stimulus to raising achievement in boys.

All skills, geographical or otherwise, need rehearsing.

Urban Transport in Newcastle-upon-Tyne

Context

In the run-up to GCSE examinations (NEAB syllabus C), Y11 classes had recently attempted a past exam question about traffic management. The last part of the question called for an explanation of an integrated transport management scheme. Yet, with central Newcastle as a case study behind them, even the more able pupils really struggled to explain how one scheme connected with, complemented or provided an alternative to others. I tried **Maps From Memory** at the start of a three week revision programme to boost their confidence.

This 100 minute lesson was with a mixed ability class containing a good proportion of very keen and able pupils among whom girls outnumbered boys. We first went over a few of the exam questions to see what was needed to get the marks available for the extended writing parts of the higher tier paper. They were ready for something active and they enjoyed it enough to voluntarily suggest other opportunities in the syllabus where we could use it again. I thought it was an excellent idea that they should take a constructive role in the revision programme. After all, they knew better than I did what they felt they needed help with.

> This is a formative response that tries a different approach to the subject matter.

Preparation

I drew a sketch map of the integrated transport scheme of central Newcastle on a large flip chart. It was extensively labelled and used colours and symbols which were identified in a key. The flip chart stand was located in a corner of the room well away from the tables and facing away from them. *Resource 1* can be enlarged onto A3 paper or alternatively you can make an OHT copy and project it onto a free-standing screen facing away from the class. Given that this resource is in black and white, you would be well advised to apply colours yourself using felt or ohp pens. Once done, it can be reused indefinitely.

Pupils seated themselves around tables in friendship groups of threes and fours as usual, a format I know works well. If it didn't, I would probably spread the more able or less well motivated pupils around the groups. You will know what works for you.

> Successful group work can depend on the teacher knowing the class well. It is also a means to getting to know them well!

I made sure that all exercise and textbooks were out of the way. Each table was equipped with a blank sheet of flip chart paper (light coloured sugar paper would do just as well) and a pack of coloured felt-tipped pens of the 'painting stick' type. I had a box of drawing pins for instruction 5 below. And that is all that was needed.

Launching

This began along the lines of: '*Having drawn loads of maps and diagrams in your books over the last year and a half, I'd hate you to discover that you'd wasted your time just when you might need to bring them to mind when it most matters - in the exam. Even if you aren't asked to draw one, if you can see it in your mind's eye and remember what it's all about you'll be able to write about it. I bet you've had to remember and draw labelled diagrams of the equipment you'd need in a science experiment before now, so you know you can do this sort of thing with practice*'. There were some mutterings about not being able to do those either from the more self-deprecating in the class.

> Self-esteem and confidence are significant variables in pupils' capacity to learn.

Every person in each group was given a number 1 to 3 or 1 to 4 and told that each person in number order would come to the corner to look at the sketch map on the flip chart for 20 seconds only, then return to their table to draw as much as they could remember for 2 minutes. When I shouted '*Next*' the following person would come out to the flip chart and so on. This was my own first run through this activity and there will be some readers with the vision to predict that there was a need for stiffer ground rules.

I told them that there was a sketch map of the integrated transport scheme in Newcastle on the flip chart drawn in colour and I gave them a minute to discuss how they might go about the task. I could hear one group talking about how they did jigsaw puzzles by doing the edges first and another talking about taking responsibility for different colours.

> Pupils here are transferring a strategy unprompted.

Instructions

1 I told all the number 1s to come to the corner with the flip chart and everyone else to remain in their chairs.

2 The 1s were shown the sketch map for 20 seconds then the flip chart cover sheet was pulled down over it.

3 After 2 minutes I shouted '*Number 2s next*' over the chatter and showed them the map in the same way.

4 I continued this until it was clear that most groups were in the process of making alterations to earlier contributions rather than adding much in the way of new information. On this occasion I allowed 6 visits to the flip chart so that everyone had been up at least once.

5 Groups were told to add the names of their team members to their drawing and then to pin it to the wall for judging.

Managing the activity

The potential for bedlam and 'professional fouls' quickly became evident. Firstly, having announced the title of the map, one particularly able group began to draw straight away, so I stopped them and warned them that it just might be a different kind of map to the one they knew and made reference to the topological style of the Tyneside Metro / London Underground map compared with a road map. That seemed to do the trick at least until the game got underway.

Secondly, in the hubbub one group could poach from another. When I warned them that others might see what they have drawn, they got into tighter huddles and the noise level dropped! I instituted a penalty of a one minute delay of release at the end of the lesson for anyone leaving their group out of turn.

Although I had said I would give each drawer 20 seconds to look at the flip chart I just estimated it. Likewise, the 2 minutes for drawing were guessed. It was less when I could see that a drawer had run out of steam but I didn't ever allow much more than 2 minutes in order to ensure that all team members made significant contributions to the map. I gave time warnings now and then to maintain momentum though it wasn't really needed. As you can imagine, there was less frantic drawing and more discussion of detail as the activity progressed.

Between visits to the flip chart, I meandered around the groups to eavesdrop and note the strategies they were using to build their map. This was useful for prompting memories during debriefing.

> This form of monitoring is natural to most teachers. It is diagnostic in that it tells you more about pupils' learning than the end product does.

> The group had become progressively better listeners and contributors over time.

Debriefing

This took almost as long as the activity partly because by Y11 these confident, enthusiastic pupils were used to debriefing and secondly because they seemed to be aware that we were discussing something that could be useful to them in other subjects that involved graphical representation.

I started by asking if the approach they had decided on before the first person went up to the flip chart had been a good one. Several groups said they had decided to wait and see what it was about first. One group of four had begun by quartering their A3 paper with one person being responsible for each. However:

'*Dividing it up didn't really work. You had too many things to remember and you needed all the colours.*' Another added: '*Some things, like the Metro, were like, really obvious and you could do that first and then fit on the other bits.*'

I said I had heard how some teams had started telling the next person to go up what to look for. Could they remember what those things were? A couple had done it by colour, but others had said '*Do the bus things*' and '*Look at the writing by the…*' One group had been allocated specific tasks by the first, and somewhat confident person, who had effectively deconstructed the map by having studied the key and told the others to do the metro, the writing, the roads.

When I asked which had been the easy and which the hard parts to remember there was general agreement that the labelling had been harder than the mapping, despite the fact that a good number of them had said they couldn't remember maps when we had been debriefing the exam earlier in the lesson.

They all agreed that they had worked as teams rather than individuals and that they hadn't simply drawn lines and labelled. They'd talked *about* what the map showed as they gave each other advice. One group had organised themselves into taking charge of a form of transport each and then shared out the labelling jobs by colour. Not surprisingly, they said that the wording of the labels was easiest to remember if it was something they already knew and understood. Those that were highlighted in colour had stood out of the sketch map and helped them memorise them.

I was interested to know if they could see how this activity might help them with their revision. One useful idea was that it could be useful to convert their notes of some topics into diagrammatic form and then revise from that. The idea of highlighting key words and phrases wasn't entirely unknown to them but they did appreciate that that can be very effective as well. I was hoping that someone would say that the activity made them look carefully at what each component of the map represented. When I suggested it they said that it was obvious, though I have my doubts that it was for everyone.

So could the class think of other case studies that they could map in a similar way to this one? Someone eventually suggested the issues surrounding the Aswan Dam scheme in Egypt and we discussed how a labelled sketch map might be constructed. Everyone agreed to begin with a base map of the route of the Nile, the dam and the Mediterranean coast, then to locate Cairo and to shade in the areas of dense population. One pupil suggested that the advantages and disadvantages could be put around the outside of the map with arrows pointing to the relevant places. Another said it would help them to remember the labels if advantages and disadvantages were in different colours.

A second useful topic that they suggested was that of migration from Mexico to California with the line across a page to represent the border with the pull and push factors in different colours above and below it. Potential obstacles to migration such as limits on the number of work permits, border patrols, language and so on could be put along the border.

They came up with several other ideas which need not take up space here. The pupils were collectively trawling through the catalogue of topics studied looking for labelled sketch mapping opportunities which suggested that they might well construct their own in the revision process. Time would tell.

I was hooked on the strategy. We had all enjoyed the lesson and it had clearly impressed one of the girls who, on the way out, said, *'Good lesson Sir'*. Now that doesn't happen every day!

A Key Skill is well developed in this group. It comes with practice. Hence opportunities for groupwork should be regular features of the classroom.

This kind of transformation connects the two sides of the brain.

Pupils here are engaged in the transfer of ideas between contexts.

This episode indicates that pupils are beginning to think of sketch maps as mental models.

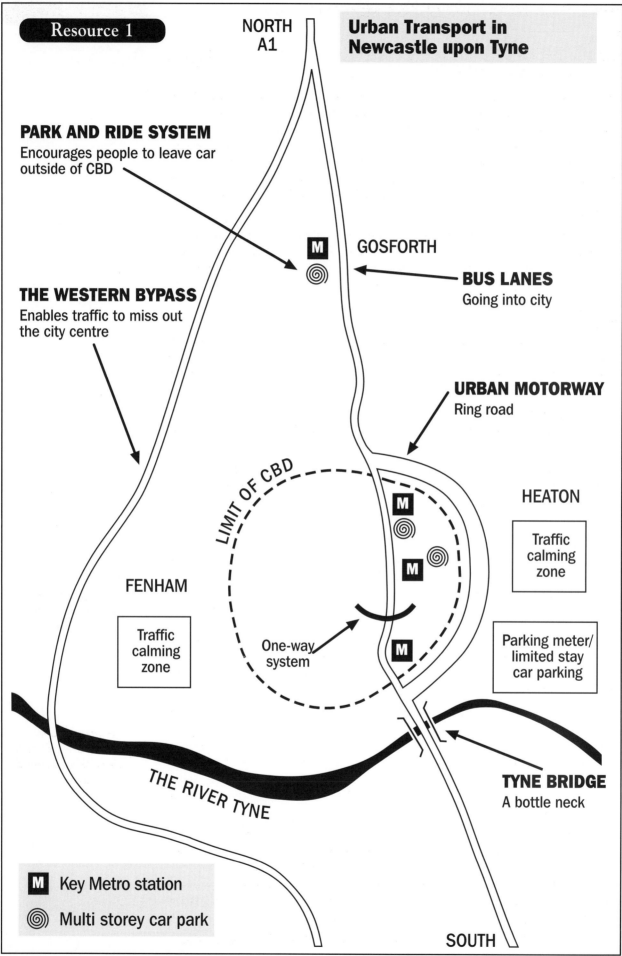

Resource 1

NORTH
A1

Urban Transport in Newcastle upon Tyne

PARK AND RIDE SYSTEM
Encourages people to leave car outside of CBD

THE WESTERN BYPASS
Enables traffic to miss out the city centre

GOSFORTH

BUS LANES
Going into city

URBAN MOTORWAY
Ring road

LIMIT OF CBD

HEATON

Traffic calming zone

FENHAM

Traffic calming zone

One-way system

Parking meter/ limited stay car parking

THE RIVER TYNE

TYNE BRIDGE
A bottle neck

Ⓜ Key Metro station

◎ Multi storey car park

SOUTH

Note: This map is neither comprehensive nor to scale!

The British Isles - Using KS3 Map D

Context

Which mountaineer was it who, when asked why he wanted to climb a particular peak, replied, 'Because it's there'? I forget.

I'd be interested to know how other teachers use the NC maps, if at all. *The British Isles* KS3 one in particular doesn't seem to have that 'fitness of purpose' to make it particularly useful. It was included, after all, to be a summary of the basic locational knowledge of features and places pupils should know by the end of KS3, rather than a map to be used during the study of rivers or uplands or whatever, for which an atlas map is much better. None the less, stung by criticism from a parent once that her son didn't seem to know where anywhere was (anywhere?) I tried the NC map D with **Maps From Memory** 'because it's there'.

The somewhat high spirited group was a mixed ability Y7 class and the 40 minute lesson came only a few weeks into the autumn term at a time when I was consciously seeking to provide positive experiences of both geography in the High School and 'Thinking' lessons in particular. I did have one or two concerns about keeping order, my relationship with the class being still in its formative phase!

Preparation

This was simplicity itself. Before the lesson, I replaced a wall map of the UK, which showed most of the features of KS3 map D, with a poster, but I left a satellite image in place. I wondered if anyone would notice and make use of it to help with the coastline or to recognise or interpret upland areas, which were distinctly visible across the classroom.

The only modification I made to map D was to add the River Tyne and mark on our town. I have learned never to overestimate pupils' ability to locate where they live! I suggest you add your own selection of local features but take care not to overcrowd the map.

I made two photocopies of the map because if the map is as small as A4 there is too much crowding when pupils gather round to look at it. I also printed off enough for one per group for use later. (see *Debriefing*) The room was arranged for groupings of four, each group with plain A4 paper and a pencil.

Launching

The class arrived pleased to see the room arranged for group activities. I think that comforts some Y7 pupils. After all, it was only the previous year that almost all their classroom work was organised in such a manner. I told them that today's lesson would involve memory, drawing skills and teamwork. They sat in groups of four and one of three without much fuss. I began with a few quick-fire questions on what I call 'Guinness' knowledge (the sort of things you find in the *Guinness Book of Records*, that pupils of this age love) such as highest mountains, longest rivers, furthest points, biggest cities and so on, as scene setters. They did quite well at naming these but asked if they could locate these features on a map, they avoided my eyes, tellingly.

Before getting the activity underway, I asked them to discuss how they were going to attempt the activity. I made the point that if they could work out an effective way to do it, then they could use it again another time, in any lesson and even when they are on their own. I soon realised the need to inform them that the map had no colours. Knowing it to be a map of the UK I could hear most groups agreeing to do the coastline first. One group's strategy was to wait and see the map first. Another looked keenly at the satellite image which gave a big hint to the others!

Instructions

I asked the groups to number each pupil 1 - 4 (or 1-3 in one case) and told them that each would come out one at a time in number order to look carefully at a map, then return to their group and draw what they could remember. Each person should add to what previous people had drawn. They were allowed to alter it if they wanted to make the map more accurate. (At this point, I quickly gave out erasers!)

Each person would have 15 seconds to study the UK map and two minutes each to draw.

> Fortunately, this is also NC geography KS3 knowledge too!

> Listening to pupils' discussions provides a basic resource for the debriefing phase later.

Managing the activity

There were some hairy moments which, in retrospect, I could have managed better and have done so since!

Clearly, 15 seconds wasn't enough to look at and interpret the map and there was some indignation expressed by number ones (ie, complaints) when I hid map D from view, and most returned to their groups and started drawing outlines by referring to the satellite image on the wall. Next time, that goes too! I gave the others between 20 and 30 seconds to study map D. 'Not fair' cried the number ones! Life isn't fair, I thought to myself.

It got a bit noisy once or twice as pupils shouted instructions to each other, argued or tried to grab the pencil from its rightful user. I had to introduce 'an official drawer only' rule which calmed them down.

After the fourth person to go had drawn for their two minutes I stopped them and asked them to nominate someone who should go again who could best finish the drawing. This led to a squabble in one group, but at least it showed enthusiasm! This was something that could have been sorted out before the start.

One boy skipped his turn and was found drawing (with great accuracy) characters from South Park on a piece of paper from his homework book. I told him to go next, but hadn't taken notice of what had already been drawn or the discussion surrounding it and his contribution to the group's drawing was in danger of being more of a hindrance than a help, so I moved him to the teacher's table for the remainder of the activity.

I stopped them when the groups looked as if they had run out of steam or were making adjustments rather than additions.

Debriefing

This fell into two related phases: assessment; and reflection on how they did it. I had originally thought of pinning their maps up on the wall for judging but realised that to see them properly there would be bedlam, so I asked them to consider three aspects of their maps that they ought to be judged by. (I thought using a term like 'assessment criteria', would be pushing my luck with Y7.) The first and predictable response was 'neatness'. (There is a strong consciousness about this aspect of pupils' work among those from particular feeder primary schools, I find.) 'Whether it's right or not' and 'If it's all there' were offered and so we agreed that accuracy, detail and neatness would be fine.

I asked them to score themselves out of 5 for each criterion and suggest ways in which they could have achieved a higher score for themselves. One common point to emerge was that they needed to dwell for much longer looking at the map to appreciate, interpret and establish the inter-relationships between the components of the map. (My words!) They also needed time to associate the meanings of the labels with those of the marked features. This is a really valid point. In the **rationale** of this chapter we say we are trying to encourage these very things if the activity isn't to be any more than a memorising of pretty (or ugly) points and patterns, and they must be given enough time. Another interesting point made by one of the more able boys was that 'Neatness isn't worth much if it's wrong!' Scores for accuracy and detail seemed to relate to how hurriedly they had tried to draw the map - another argument against a competitive dimension, I suppose.

Most groups thought that if you didn't get the coastline 'right' then you couldn't possibly position other features accurately. A further problem for them was the size of pupils' writing for labels compared with the printed version. Large lettering caused a bit of confusion and some felt that if there was a word on part of the map, they couldn't put any other feature there.

This led us into the second phase of the **debriefing.** I was really pleased that as an outcome of the previous discussions, they suggested that next time, they would make an effort to get the coastline (or whatever form the 'base map' might be) drawn as well as possible first and to leave the words until last. Was I deluding myself in thinking that here were signs of real understanding of what maps are about?

As much of the learning in TT lessons takes place in a social context, there will always be some pupils who have difficulty with working collaboratively. In the long term, this Key Skill will only develop by regular engagement, not removal from it. It could be argued that pupils lacking in this skill need more not less exposure to it.

This hits NCTS Evaluation, Improving Own Learning and Performance spot on. The pupils are also using metacognition.

Pupils have to decide what is important. An appreciation of the process of map making grows out of this.

Destructive Plate Margins

Context

Although the **rationale** at the start of this chapter focuses on teaching and learning about maps, most is equally relevant to diagrams. As simplified models of structures or processes pupils need to understand and not merely reproduce them and with this particular topic, given the added complication (or in some cases obstacle) of technical terminology, understanding the diagrams supports the understanding of the processes involved. Pupils often remember the diagram, some the terms and some the processes, but I still get a buzz when they can pull all three threads together.

This topic is first introduced towards the end of Y8 and is revisited at GCSE in Y11 where I have also used **Maps From Memory**. This Exemplar describes the first half of a 40 minute lesson with a middle band group of 27 pupils near the start of a unit on volcanoes which began by using **5W** to generate **enquiry** questions such as 'Where are they? Why do they happen? and Why are they different?' This was followed by an exercise locating volcanoes using latitude and longitude on a world map with plate boundaries marked. (You all know the exercise!) They knew little more than the association between volcanoes and plate boundaries and that the earth's crust is broken into pieces called plates. This activity was to help begin thinking about the Why? questions and to familiarise them with key terminology.

Preparation

Choose a diagram carefully. Some are decidedly vague in the sub-continental zone. I used Waugh's diagram in *The Wider World* (p 212) in class. This is in colour and you have to decide in advance if you want the groups to draw theirs in monochrome and thereby add an extra dimension to the challenge but simplify the management of equipment, or to go for technicolour and risk spending your break picking up coloured pencils! The other risk is that pupils can get diverted by colouring in rather than adding features or labels. If you want black and white, enlarge the diagram on the photocopier. This can be helpful to pupils who are short sighted or colour blind. I'm sure there are more than we ever get to know about.

> Pupils with other disabilities, especially immobility, should be considered with this activity.

Thereafter, preparation was the same as for the other Exemplars. The class was used to working collaboratively. Visual memory, interpretation ability and drawing skills are all involved in this activity and friendship groups usually seem to contain a good enough mix for there not to be predictable 'winners'.

Each group was given one ordinary and four coloured pencils and a piece of plain A4 paper.

Launching

This class has experienced **Maps From Memory** twice before and they call it 'the drawing game' and when I announced it, I'm sure I could hear someone whisper 'Yes! No writing!' Enough said.

I said that this time they would have to draw diagrams instead of maps, and that these are useful diagrams to help explain why volcanoes occur where they do. I complimented them (as a reminder) on how well they had done last time. This was disputed by one group, which claimed that theirs had been **** and this seemed to be a good opportunity to think about which approaches had and hadn't been useful. One group remembered that dividing up the map into quarters had not only been difficult for 'connecting bits together' but it had been unfair too. There were unequal amounts of map information in each quarter! Another group remembered dividing up responsibility for drawing and labelling. I gave them a minute or so to decide what approach to take this time, and pointed out that there were in fact two diagrams to draw. I told them that we would talk about how they did it afterwards.

> And perhaps which kind of language is appropriate in this setting!

> Pupils' evaluation of their own previous strategies is part of the metacognitive process.

Instructions

These were as for *Exemplar 2* but included nominating their 'best' drawer to go again at the end. I also said that only one person at a time could draw, with the sanction of missing a turn if a group broke that rule. (Lookouts were posted!)

Managing the activity

This hardly needed managing: they were so engaged. When they saw that there were two diagrams, groups started to reconsider strategies, something to be picked up in **debriefing**.

My only intervention was to warn some of them about holding on to pencils when it wasn't their turn to draw.

It took nearly 20 minutes for the full cycle of five visits to the front (four plus the 'best' drawer again) and I stopped the drawing when I could see seagulls, Titanics and other trivia being added!

Debriefing

Sometimes classes find this reflective process difficult but this class has become quite used to it. To my opening question, whether it was harder or easier than the previous map from memory, there was a divided response. Some thought the map had been easier because the outline had been familiar; some found the diagram easier because they knew a bit about it already; others, quite the reverse, because they had little or no knowledge of it. Despite previous discussion about strategies, one group had agreed to divide the diagram into quarters but was thwarted by the linear nature of the diagrams. Sensibly, one group changed its approach to working from left to right across the diagrams, which had worked well until reaching the edge of the A4 paper! It had been successful apart from that problem. The other reverted to a simple model: one drawer and one labeller for each diagram. Equal success.

I was interested that only three groups put titles to their diagrams, and that was the last thing they did, as if it was an afterthought. So I asked them to turn their drawing face down and to tell me what the diagrams showed. Amidst the plethora of 'sort of's, 'like's and 'thing's, between them they constructed a pretty good explanation of what was going on in the diagram, including a sense that the arrows indicated motion. There was some good use of the terminology too.

I asked them how they could summarise what the diagrams were about. Someone volunteered the title from the book though few had given their diagrams a title at all. My fault. I had said to draw the diagram and they took it literally. Even so, we agreed it was a good idea to notice the title because it tells you what the diagram is about. Similar comments emerged about the key. Starting by looking for titles and the keys of maps and diagrams may seem blindingly obvious, but on the evidence of these classroom experiences, not to everyone. Are adults any better, I wonder?

Follow-up

From time to time, pupils engaged with *thinking skills* activities ask what the point is. Since the class had already generated their own sequence of enquiry questions that this activity had addressed, pupils already knew that their next steps were closely linked to what had been going on in class. I had a range of texts, photocopied newspaper reports and print-offs from web pages available for them to write up their responses to the question 'Why do volcanoes occur?' This was then included in their enquiry reports.

Afterthoughts

As with most *thinking skills* activities there is no one single 'right' answer to the tasks, though in **Maps From Memory** an accurately drawn and complete map is a 'right answer'. However, that misses the point, which is to think about, test and evaluate strategies to aid recognition and memory, recall and understanding – and these are numerous. Pupils, of course, want you to *tell* them what the best way is. We don't like to do this in our department. We don't completely agree! So at best if asked, we might say 'Have you tried...?' or 'What if you did things in a different order?'

This activity succeeds best if the pupils work as a group: that is, they collaborate, discuss, ask questions of each other and guide each other. It can be that one dominant person in a group calls all the shots and that isn't easy to regulate, so the strategy is not without its weak spots. There is a strong case for giving more time to look and less time to draw as long as the seated members don't become restless while their teammate is studying the map for detail.

I don't find **debriefing** very easy, partly because, while I'm fairly sure what strategies work for me, I'm not approaching the situation from, say, a Y7's perspective. They tend to want firm solutions and answers while I want them to be thinking freely, speculating and testing ideas and ways of doing things, and feeling confident enough to take risks. That was one reason for letting them evaluate their own maps rather than expose them to public

The willingness of groups to change approaches mid-stream varies considerably. It indicates flexibility of thinking.

Pupils frequently omit titles to maps and diagrams that they draw in their books. It may be an indication that they have not actually engaged with the meaning and purpose of their drawing.

Ambiguity is a strong characteristic of many *TTG* activities. It provokes thinking.

We do not all think at the same speed. Allowing enough thinking time enables more pupils to participate and therefore can be construed to be a form of differentiation.

comparison. They knew what a 'perfect' map looked like anyway. I realise that this viewpoint is in opposition to the use of competition that we also employ from time to time as a spur to effort. As *thinking skills* practitioners frequently say, there isn't only one right solution. It's a matter of professional judgement!

Adapting the strategy

If you have a good rapport with the class, try instituting a rule that the pupil who has been out to see the diagram / map is the one not allowed to draw, but must *describe* to the others what to draw.

Good groupwork skills are needed for this.

In this chapter the strategy has been described in the context of maps and diagrams. It is a small step to using photographs in a similar manner to develop observing, describing, listening and drawing skills and imagination. As such it has strong links with the **Reading Photographs** strategy in *TTG*. Pupils can come to the teacher to study a picture then return to draw it until the group can suggest what it is, or they can try and describe it to others in the group to draw with following members in turn adding detail. Alternatively, as a paired activity one person looks at and describes to their partner a map, picture, diagram or even graph. This can work well for those artefacts that geographers typically bring back in their suitcases from their holidays!

More Thinking Through Geography

Chapter 4

Making Animals

4 Making Animals

Rationale

This is a really fun way of applying geographical understanding of environments and processes, natural or human to given situations. Given an environment and starting with a 'clean slate' in evolutionary terms, what might be the 'perfect' adaptation of an animal to, say the tundra environment? What environmental factors would the animal have to cope with? – daylight? seasonal temperatures? plant growth? How could it be adapted to these conditions? – hibernation? camouflage? protection? What could it look like? This is **Making Animals** in its simplest form.

Exemplars 2 and 3 are more complex, as is a fourth *Exemplar* which can be downloaded from **www.chriskingtonpublishing.co.uk.** These are planning and decision making exercises where pupils are required to use criteria based upon their knowledge and experience to reach conclusions. The idea of criteria is also important to geography. The activities encourage pupils to consider how their minds are working and how other people approach planning and decision making.

Making Animals needs parameters or constraints: environments, political systems, or preferences for herbivores / omnivores of the rainforest. Students need to plan their decisions as they need to fit the constraints / criteria that they have been given by the teacher. These should not be so restrictive as to shackle imagination and creativity, or too open such that everything is possible. Life isn't like that. The **Layered Decision Making** Exemplars work in this way too.

Two important aspects to **Making Animals** will be concentrated on: firstly, pupils' growing understanding of planning and decision making; and secondly, how it can be used as an assessment tool.

These are two of geography's Big Concepts. Essentially, this is a decision-making strategy.

Understanding about planning development in **Making Animals** can be transferred to many other contexts

Making Animals and Plants

Context

This activity has been used with KS3 pupils in different schools both in mixed ability sets and in setted classes. It has been used in a module on climate and vegetation zones and a module dealing specifically with Alaska. I also know of teachers who have used it successfully to introduce the idea of climate zones and ecosystems at A Level.

This particular lesson was used with a Y9 class of very mixed ability when they were looking at tropical rainforest ecosystems. They had previously studied the characteristics of rainforest environments so were familiar with the climate, diurnal weather pattern and forest structure. The class was used to working in groups, as many of their previous lessons had required this. There were one or two 'characters' in the group who could be difficult in behaviour terms.

Preparation

Normally the tables are set out for groups of four but I rearranged them for working in pairs to ensure that all pupils would be involved.

Pupils needed their exercise books, the sheet of animal characteristics (*Resource 1*) – which can be reused for any natural environment – and the criteria or constraints that they will be planning within (given below). Each pair was given a photograph of the rainforest, a diagram showing the different vegetation layers, a climate graph and a piece of A4 paper. A suitable textbook would do as an alternative. I also put an OHT of a typical cross section of tropical rainforest on the screen once the activity was underway.

Launching

This lesson often starts badly as many of the pupils are coming from a PE lesson and are frequently late and a little 'high'. It can often take them a little while to settle. Prior to them arriving I had put a picture of a shark onto the screen using an OHP. (This had been prepared using Bubble Jet Transparencies, a colour printer and the Internet - a fantastic resource for teachers.) The picture had the statement 'The perfect animal' underneath it. I stood at the door and greeted the students as they arrived in dribs and drabs telling them to get their books out and to write a response to the picture and statement on the screen. Many of them actually wrote a good paragraph in response to this visual stimulus.

I gave them a minute after everybody had arrived and then started a whole class discussion about the picture and statement. There were many interesting and varied responses including some excellent ones from one of the difficult pupils who had actually written nothing but had obviously been thinking about it. I eventually twisted the discussion to the idea of characteristics (without too much effort). We had frequently talked about these in debriefing sessions in relation to describing and comparing.

Instructions

The students were told that for the main part of their lesson they would have to design an animal to meet the simple description or criteria that they are given. Each pair was given one of two animals:

> *A carnivore that lives in the rainforest*
> *or*
> *A herbivore that lives in the rainforest*

I told them to pick one of the 2 kinds of animals then use the list of characteristics to choose which they thought might be appropriate characteristics for it. If they felt the need for a characteristic not listed they needed to ask me for permission. This 'constraint' was to prevent their animals being fitted with force fields and laser guided rockets. However, I did tell them that their animal did not have to be like any existing animals as long as it could survive. I told them what a prehensile tail was.

I next told them to write down the selected characteristics in the back of their books as a working list. Before starting, I reinforced the point that the object was not to design a super creature from outer space that could take over the world, but one that could survive or thrive in its environment. I reminded them of some of the comments that they had made about the shark: well equipped for its marine environment; but would not survive in many other environments.

Once they had written their list of characteristics I asked them to visualise the animal that they had designed, using the **Mind Movie** technique: How big is it? How does it move, find food, hide, defend itself, communicate, and rest? I steered clear of reproduction for obvious reasons, though it may have crossed some minds. I then asked them to write a description of their creature, explaining and justifying its characteristics. They were reminded to use and refer to the pictures and climate graph. I gave them a final opportunity to make changes to the characteristics.

If they finished their writing, they were set the task of drawing their animal.

Management

This is a form of scaffolding where the critical feature of the task is highlighted. It is also immediate feedback which informs learning.

The class was really enthusiastic but the imaginations of some pairs ran a little wild, and so I stopped the class once when I realised that a couple of groups were not really thinking about the constraints of the type of animal, climate or forest structure. I used the following analogy: *'Those purple jeans may look great but they do not really match the orange blouse you want to wear to the School Prize Evening. You have to 'fit the occasion' and the environment. In the forest, do you want to be noticed, or camouflaged? Do you really need wings if you find your food on the forest floor? Think about it!'* Other than this, little management was necessary, as the class were all really enjoying the activity.

This is a further example of feedback, this time from peers.

An indication that they were finishing their drawings was that they started taking a lot of interest in those of other pairs. It got a bit noisy but, apart from good fun, I could hear some design characteristics being challenged such as 'What use are feet like that if it lives in trees?' They were obviously being forced to think harder about habitat and adaptation.

Debriefing

To help students understand how they plan and make decisions, I began debriefing simply:

'How do you decide what to wear when you go out on a Saturday night?'

This confirms decision-making as a transferable skill.

This led to a discussion of the role of factors and characteristics and other contexts in geography where they are important (eg, route planning, redevelopment schemes, dam building). I asked them if they needed to make decisions in other subjects. In one way or another, they argued that they did in all of them.

Characteristics are also brought into the fore in **Most Likely To....**

I then changed the debrief focus to characteristics. When I asked why characteristics were important in geography one pupil said you could not describe things if you did not know what the characteristics of that thing were. To illustrate this I asked one sceptical boy to describe somebody else without using any characteristics. He tried valiantly but every time he started the rest of the class would shout out that he was using a characteristic in his description. Case proven and one very satisfied teacher.

Adapting the simple version

This activity has also been used in the same way for **Making Plants**. A list of characteristics *(Resource 2)* is included for you. The niche the plant occupies in the ecosystem can be defined by you in the same way as the animals could be herbivores or omnivores. Here are a few suggested parameters for pupils to work to:

A plant that provides safety for animals

A plant that provides food for animals

A plant that can resist fire

A plant that depends on animals to reproduce itself

A sunlight loving plant

A shade loving plant

The exercise has also been successfully used as **Making Houses** for different climatic zones. At A Level this could even be applied to smaller scale ecosystems eg, sand dunes, moorland peat bogs, and water meadows.

Making Animals

Choose from the list of animal characteristics below to design an animal adapted to the natural environment that you have been given. You will be told about one or more important characteristics which the animal *must* have. Consult your teacher if you think your animal should have additional characteristics that are not listed. They must be characteristics that could occur in the natural world.

fast runner	can get fat	powerful digging claws
migratory	thick skin	spotted fur
can stand on 2 legs	large ears	long neck
striped fur	sharp claws	grinding teeth
sharp incisor teeth	swims	thick fur
climbs trees	thick pads on paws	nocturnal
good eyesight	webbed feet	can hibernate
can close nostrils	agile	slippery skinned
good sense of smell	gives off bad smell	stores water in body
strong skeleton	loud voice	gregarious (lives in groups)
stamina	brown fur	prehensile (gripping) tail
large body	very thin body	whiskers
can hold breath for ½ hour	sociable	fierce growl

Resource 2 — Making Plants

Choose from the list of plant characteristics below to design a plant adapted to the natural environment that you have been given. You will be told about one or more important characteristics which the plant *must* have. Consult your teacher if you think your plant should have additional characteristics that are not listed. They must be characteristics that could occur in the natural world.

drought resistant	loves water	stores water
wide root system	deep root system	lives on other plants
floats	survives under water	dies back seasonally
waxy, pointed leaves	deciduous	evergreen
broadleaves	needle leaves	stunted (close to ground)
thick bark	rough bark	wind-blown seeds
heavy-weight seeds	fragments take root	seeds with velcro-like hooks
runners put down roots	climber	likes strong sun
likes shade	tall	salt tolerant
bears fruit (nuts & berries)	flowering	pollinating
eats insects	branching	sticks to rocks
lifecycle within days	colourful	drab
pleasant smell	awful smell	changes colour
buttress roots	flexible branches	sticky surfaces

Migration - Packing for a Journey

Context

This activity, designed by a PGCE student as a course requirement was used as a Y9 assessment with classes in the middle of a large unit looking at the USA, focusing on Mexican migration into California. The class described was able and responsive to other TTG activities. They sometimes got a little boisterous and needed putting back on task but were confident contributors to debriefing episodes.

> This class generally has a broad conception of learning and is not suspicious about 'different' learning activities.

Preparation

Print copies of *Resources 3 and 4*, at least one per group.

Atlases were put onto desks prior to pupils arriving. No mention of these was made. Even when I was asked a direct question, I only said that they were there to use if needed.

Launching

On entry to the room, the pupils were handed a copy of *Resource 3*, a section of a story about Pedro Morales, a Mexican migrating to California. Once everyone was in the room and (most) had read the story, I asked a few questions to establish connections with previous work which had used a photo of a migrant crawling under the border fence and a sequence from the video of Michael Palin's *Pacific Journey*.

> The photo may encourage those with strong visual / spatial skills. It will generally jog memory and thinking.

Instructions

Pupils were put into groups of around four and told that they were the Morales family and had to decide what Pedro would take on his journey to California. *Resource 4* lists the items they may choose for Pedro to take, but limited by what he could carry. I told them their written up decisions and justifications would be assessed and that discussing their reasoning would be a good idea.

Managing the activity

This able group needed little managing, except for me to go around each group to check on progress and to note down interesting comments for the debriefing session. While working, I often asked why they were taking a certain piece of equipment, to encourage them to be prepared to give a reason or justification.

Debriefing

Quoting comments I had noted down, I asked two groups to explain their choices of particular items to the class which was warned to listen carefully as they would be evaluating the explanations. They needed to identify what was good, or how it could have been better. Constructive ideas were welcomed as being helpful for the assessment. All except one person reacted well to the criticism. (However, this one basically just dug his heels in.) The most positive comments were directed at the extending reasoning for taking a particular item: offering a reason for a reason, if you like. For example the first student said that he would take matches to light a fire because he needed to keep warm and cook dinner. The class said that this was a good explanation because a reason was given (use of 'because' was praised). I said that I kept warm and cooked without using matches. After some 'buts' and 'thats' – 'cos' one girl contributed *'he needed to keep warm because he might have to survive outside in a desert where it gets cold at night and he would need a fire to cook on if he were outside'*. Excellent reasoning.

> This is another example of debriefing providing feedback which is probably far more effective than written comments in books. It is Assessment for Learning.

Follow-up

The write–up of their decisions was a homework exercise to be formally assessed and put into their assessment file. We discussed the overall structure of the writing. It would need an introduction and the end should summarise how the combination of items would be so useful.

> Teaching Thinking generally acts as a good preparation and bridge into writing and improved literacy.

Resource 3

The Story of Pedro Morales

As immigrants from Mexico arrived, they descended on friends or relatives, where often several families were already crowded together. No one was denied a roof and food during the first days, but after a while each person had to fend for himself. They streamed in from towns south of the border, looking for work, with nothing to their names but the clothes on their backs, a bundle over their shoulders, and the will to get ahead in that 'Promised Land' where, they had been told, money grew on trees and a clever man could become very rich, with his own Cadillac and a blonde on his arm.

What they had not been told, however, was that for each success, fifty were left by the wayside and another fifty went back home defeated. They had no idea of the hardships of being away from their families, how they would be abused by some of their employers, and persecuted by the authorities looking for illegal immigrants, how much effort it would take to reunite their family, or how great the pain would be saying goodbye to their friends and leaving their dead behind. But even had they known, they might still have undertaken the journey north. Pedro Morales called himself the 'wire cutting wetback' and liked to tell the story of how many times he had crossed the border, sometimes swimming the Rio Grande and other times cutting wire fences.

At the time Pedro Morales made his first trip into California the Mexicans still had the feeling they were reclaiming territory. For them slipping across the border was not a crime but an adventure. Pedro Morales made his first trip when he was twenty; he did not want to follow in his father's and grandfather's footsteps working as a hired hand on the hacienda (farm). He decided to make the trip north into southern California to look for a job and more money.

(From *The Inevitable Plan*,
Isabel Allende,1993, HarperCollins)

KS3 Assessment

Information:

Imagine you are Pedro Morales. You are twenty years old and have decided to migrate to California in search of a well paid job. You have talked to other Mexicans who have made the trip to California before and they told you about 4 different jobs.

The task:

You have to pack for your trip. You have decided to buy the things you will need before you go because they are cheaper in Mexico. You have managed to save $40 but this will have to buy the things you will need for your trip as well. After you have decided how you will get into California, what you will take with you and what job you will do, you must write about your decisions. Your teacher will tell you more about this.

You are faced with a choice of how to cross into California. You can swim across the Rio Grande or you can cut the wires. If you swim the Rio Grande you stand a 1:10 chance of being caught; if you go under the wire then you stand a 1:3 chance of being caught. If you are caught by the Immigration Officials you can pay them a bribe of $20 and they will let you through.

Jobs:

1. Cattle ranch

The job is as a cattle hand and pays $5 a day but the work is hard and long. Your friends tell you that the ranch owner will probably want a work permit and this costs $20 but you can buy a permit after you have started working.

The ranch is in the Sacramento Mountains near to the town of El Paso. The summers are hot, dry and dusty, with temperatures around 28°C and no precipitation during the summer.

2. Fruit and cotton farm

You will be picking fruit and cotton. The work is hard and the days are long, you will be paid $2.50 a day and the farmer will employ you without a work permit.

The farm is on the Colorado river, the summer days are very hot (30°C) but there is precipitation during the summer months.

3. Factory worker

The Ford factory is in the city of San Diego close to the border with Mexico. The job pays $20 a day and the working conditions are good. You will be working inside out of the hot sun. The management of the factory will only employ workers who already have a work permit.

4. Bar work

'Caesar's Place Tacos Bar' takes on Mexicans to work on tables and behind the bar. The work is tiring and the hours are long . The pay is $2 a day but you get to keep the tips. The owner will employ you without a work permit.

Continued...

Resource 4

Shopping list in US $

Accommodation costs (B&B):

Dormitory (6 / room) 1.00
Shared (2 / room) 2.00
Own room 4.00

Cost of meals:

Breakfast 0.75
Lunch 1.00
Evening meal 2.00

Kit and clothing:

Working gloves 2.00
Safety boots 4.50
Cowboy boots 5.50
Knife 1.00
Water bottle 1.00
Socks 0.50
Pack of cards 1.00
Underwear 1.25
Shirt (smart) 2.00
Shirt (rough work) 1.00
Trousers (smart) 3.50
Trousers (rough work) 2.00
Book 2.00
Sombrero 3.00
Washing kit (toothbrush, soap etc.) 3.00
Cooking equipment (pans, plates, cutlery) 5.00
Bed roll (sleeping bag) 5.00
Jumper 2.00
Prayer beads (rosary) 0.50
Bible 2.00
Wire cutters 2.50
Matches 0.50
Cigarettes 1.00
Map 1.50
Family photo . . . .?????
Guitar 7.50

Improving a Shanty Town

Context

This version develops the decision making aspect of the strategy further. It has been used successfully as a small group activity with all our GCSE classes when looking at improving the quality of life through self-help schemes in squatter settlements on the urban / rural fringe in an ELDC. Although the ability of this particular class was mixed it was weighted towards the top end. It was one of the most enthusiastic GCSE classes I have ever taught. They were excellent at whole class discussions and responded well to debriefing sessions and seemed to gain much from them.

In previous lessons they had looked at:
- the problems and pressures in shanty towns;
- why people live in shanty towns and why they continue to migrate to the cities;
- a brief look at the different methods of improving the quality of life in shanty towns.

The exercise was designed to achieve 2 aims:
1 To allow the students to see the difficulties facing ELDCs in improving the quality of life in their less fortunate urban areas, as well as the difficulties facing the people who live in these areas in improving their own quality of life, but who still manage through ingenuity and hard work to do just this;

2 To give students an insight into the complexity of decision making. It must be done at a range of scales, short term and more long-term. Priorities need to established and justified.

The shanty town in the Exemplar is modelled on squatter settlements in general and could therefore be used in the context of any ELDC.

This took a double lesson (100 minutes) and homework.

Preparation

Print *Resources 5,6 and 8* on paper and the options for development of the shanty town (*Resource 7*) on card which should be cut up and made up into envelope sets. Students will manipulate these as they might with a **Mystery**. It has been our experience that pupils like the opportunity to change their minds without having to rewrite anything. The process of moving the pieces of paper allows them to explore meaning in an unthreatening way. It helps them to think.

> The thinking processes involved in this type of activity are explored in Leat & Nichols (1999)

Launching

I often try to start a lesson with a visual stimulus, so I projected a slide of a shanty town on the screen and had the following question written on the board 'If you lived here what daily hardships would you have to put up with?' We had a quick discussion of the problems and grouped them into categories such as health, education, living conditions and so on. Many were very keen to say that it was not clean and I eventually put another slide up showing the inside of an immaculately kept squatter settlement house to provide a different perspective.

I then wanted to think about criteria. I showed them three ways of cleaning the board. Firstly I wiped it with the duster, secondly I used my hands and thirdly I attempted to blow the chalk off the board. There was some laughter at a very red faced Scotsman. I then asked them to tell me which method was the best. '*The first one.*' '*Why?*' '*Because it was the best.*' '*Yes, but why?*' The discussion went something like:

> These launching contexts are very powerful in helping pupils to see a wider relevance to learning. They are more than fun.

'*cause it's quick*'

'*so's the hand one*'

'*it's less messy*'

'*the third one's stupid*'; '*Why?*'; '*cause it doesn't get it clean*'

...and so on. I then summarised that speed, mess and effectiveness were criteria identified for judging the three methods. We then talked about how criteria were important in evaluating a piece of work and why it was important to know them before trying to do the work. Sometimes when they say they don't know what to do, they mean they don't understand what it is that you, the teacher, are after.

> Explicit criteria are very important in developing Evaluation skills NCTS.

Instructions

The students were then told that they were elected members of the *Community of Ariba*, a well established squatter settlement in Mexico City, ie they would represent the interests of the community, not themselves alone. The residents wanted to improve the quality of life in Ariba for themselves by starting a *self help scheme*.

I gave the students the map of Ariba; the price list for improvements to a shanty town; the information sheet on shanty towns in general and on Ariba in particular; and the planning sheet. (*Resources 5, 6, 7 and 8*)

This class knows about prioritising: they do it all the time when organising their homework. So I asked them to study *Resources 5, 6 and 7* and discuss the relative importance to the community of its various problems such as crime, education, health, employment, and building quality. They then planned what their priorities would be for the 3 time periods and entered them into the 'Priorities for development' box on the planning sheet. (*Resource 8*)

They were then told to begin planning their spending of their shanty town points (STP) which, I said, had been donated by a non-governmental international development agency, but with so many real emergencies occurring around the world, there was no guarantee of more in years ahead.

Managing the activity

Once underway I had to whiz around the groups to ensure that everyone was doing the prioritisation of the problems first. As I had expected, some were already starting on the 'shopping list', so I stopped them and went through the instructions again. From then on it went smoothly.

Debriefing

My first questions were '*How did you decide on your priorities?*' and then '*Did these help with deciding how to use your STPs?*' Responses concentrated on the fact that they had read the information and discussed what were immediate needs compared to those that would be nice but could be lived without. The selection and ordering of the priorities varied between groups and this provoked some discussion about justifying their ordering. I took a back seat except on one occasion, to ask a student to listen to another before having her say. They agreed that having the priorities helped, because they could concentrate on one or two things at a time which they could manage.

Two groups found it quite frustrating that they didn't have enough STP to solve everything in one go. Some were upset that I had refused their requests for more. 'Where from?' I asked. They felt that it was unfair when their needs were so great. This triggered a very interesting discussion which raised and clarified some important issues:

- the responsibilities and abilities of Governments to help;
- ELDCs have competing priorities - perhaps industries should be helped to generate wealth first (and other arguments);
- some waste lots of money;
- Government support might only attract more migrants; should resources be spent on making the countryside 'better'?
- why does the Government not make them all leave?

Students provided all the questions and most of the answers for themselves.

I then asked which criteria were important for the people of Ariba when planning how to improve their shanty, and then how they might be different for urban planners in this country. They had already looked at inner city problems in MEDC so were building on material that they had already studied. They seemed to get the idea very well and could talk at length with the odd prompt.

Follow-up

For homework they were given the task of writing up their decisions and giving reasons for having made them. The quality of the answers was expectedly variable but all the pupils mentioned priorities in some form and justified their decisions. Many also mentioned identifying criteria as a useful part of the process.

This is complex with multi-layered demands which match NCTS requirements very strongly / closely.

Another example of scaffolding through drawing attention to the critical features of the task.

This is cognitive conflict - pupils are being challenged.

This demonstrates the value of difficult issues in stimulating pupil questioning and challenging assumptions and beliefs.

Resource 5

Key:

x x x x	Industrial area
—·—·—	Edge of shanty town
-·-·-	Dirt road track
═══	Paved road
☐	Shanty building made of wood, cardboard/ corrugated iron etc

Ariba: a shanty town

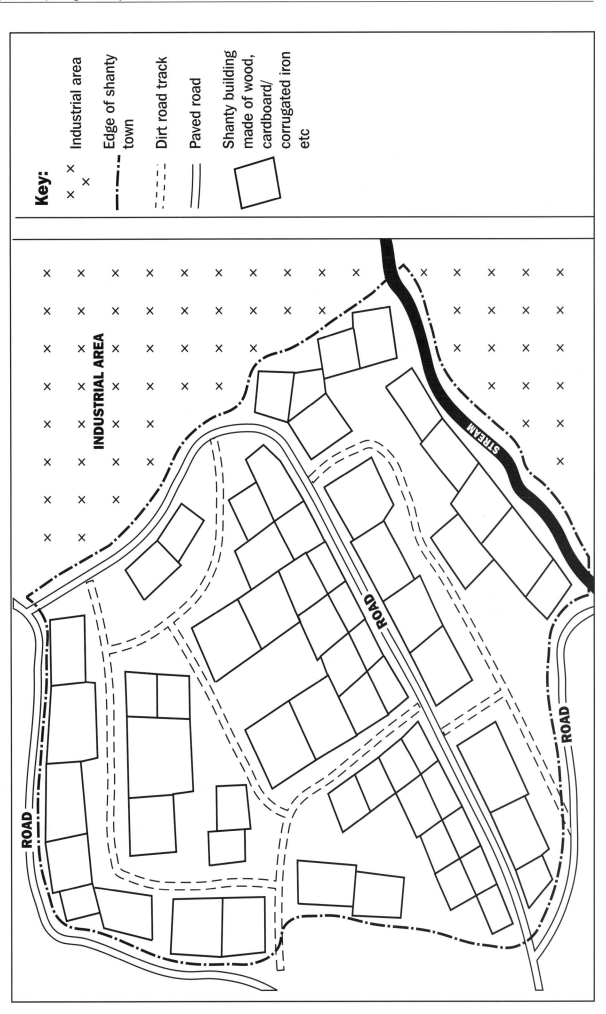

A Shanty Town

Ariba is a shanty town of poor quality, self-built houses on the fringe of a large city in Latin America. As with shanties in many less developed countries of the world, it began as temporary housing, but is becoming more permanent by the day! Most residents came from poor rural areas or country towns but with few skills of use in urban areas and little savings. Others are young adults from other poor areas of the city setting up their first homes. Unemployment is not an option. They have to do something to survive.

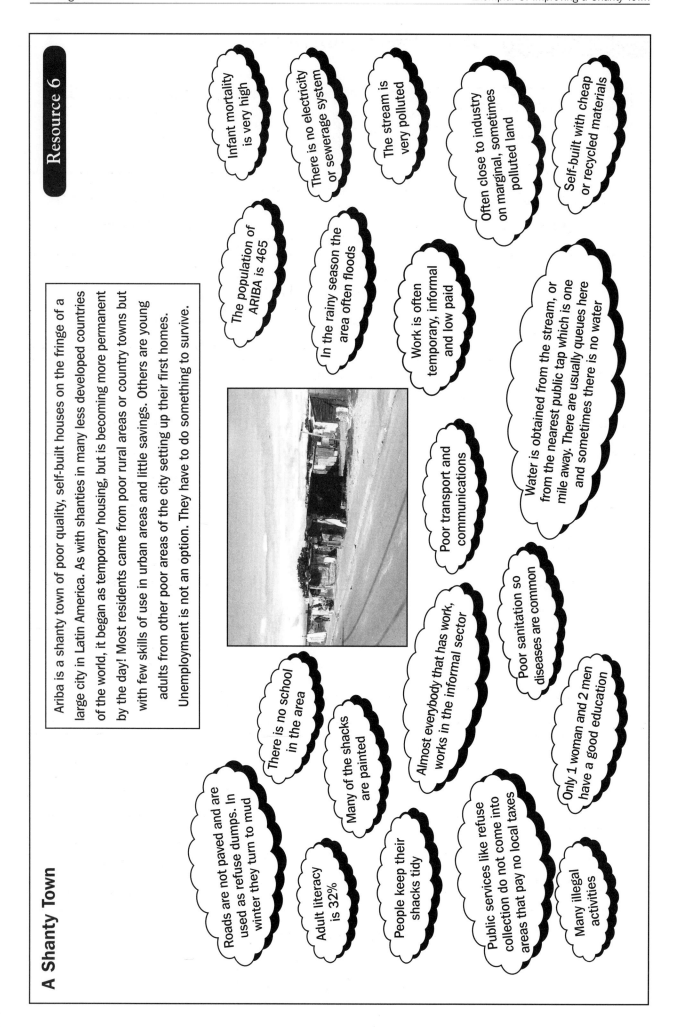

- Infant mortality is very high
- There is no electricity or sewerage system
- The stream is very polluted
- Often close to industry, sometimes on marginal, sometimes polluted land
- Self-built with cheap or recycled materials
- The population of ARIBA is 465
- In the rainy season the area often floods
- Work is often temporary, informal and low paid
- Water is obtained from the stream, or from the nearest public tap which is one mile away. There are usually queues here and sometimes there is no water
- Poor transport and communications
- Poor sanitation so diseases are common
- There is no school in the area
- Many of the shacks are painted
- Almost everybody that has work, works in the informal sector
- Only 1 woman and 2 men have a good education
- Roads are not paved and are used as refuse dumps. In winter they turn to mud
- Adult literacy is 32%
- People keep their shacks tidy
- Public services like refuse collection do not come into areas that pay no local taxes
- Many illegal activities

Resource 7   Shanty Town Improvements

STP = shanty town points   Remember you have 200 shanty town points to spend in your first year and another 200 in your second year.

100 metres of road ----------- **30 STP** -----------	Concrete for 100 metres of road ----------- **10 STP** -----------	Training for one teacher ----------- **30 STP** -----------
Prequalified teacher for a year ----------- **60 STP** -----------	Weekly doctor's visit to area ----------- **15 STP** -----------	Paint for houses ----------- **10 STP** -----------
Electricity connection for area ----------- **30 STP** -----------	Electricity connection to one building ----------- **10 STP** -----------	20 metre by 20 metre grass area ----------- **10 STP** -----------
Community centre ----------- **25 STP** -----------	Building materials for one house (concrete and wood) ----------- **10 STP** -----------	Medical supplies ----------- **20 STP** -----------
Small petrol electricity generator ----------- **20 STP** -----------	Family planning clinic ----------- **50 STP** -----------	Local factory (will employ 40 people in labouring jobs) ----------- **130 STP** -----------
Locally run health centre ----------- **35 STP** -----------	Sewerage network ----------- **100 STP** -----------	Local water tap ----------- **40 STP** -----------
Water connection per building ----------- **20 STP** -----------	Government advisor/expert for one week ----------- **40 STP** -----------	Street lighting per street ----------- **30 STP** -----------
Drainage network ----------- **100 STP** -----------	Weekly nurse's visit to area ----------- **5 STP** -----------	Send delegation to City authorities ----------- **5 STP** -----------
	Improve living conditions in the rural areas ----------- **400 STP** -----------	

Resource 8

Priorities for development
1st year
2nd year
Longer term

Improvements in 1st year	Cost	Reasons

Improvements in 2nd year	Cost	Reasons

Plans for future years

Exemplar 4

Improving a Rural Village

This is a decision making activity for KS3 though it has been used between Y7 - 11. The school has a unit involving both Brazil and Zimbabwe and an enthusiastic colleague who once visited these countries, who took charge of promoting a positive image of less developed countries. The LDM activity in class is set in Brazil. The extension work (homework) encourages the transfer of key ideas to a new context in Zimbabwe. For a full account of this strategy and for a full set of accompanying resources, go to **www.chriskingtonpublishing.co.uk**

Using Making Animals for Assessment

Having selected five to seven pieces of work that reflected the range of pupils' written responses and ranking them, we were able to identify characteristics that enabled us to develop 6 Levels of response. Although these were developed for *Exemplar 2*, they have been used for other **Making Animals** and other contexts where explaining is a major component of the responses. Typical indicators of the Levels of response of your pupils to your own version of **Making Animals** may be entered in the right hand column of *Resource 9*.

Black & Wiliam (1998) argue that formative assessment makes for significant improvement in pupil achievement. It is essential to improved performance that students are offered support, targets and advice in the light of diagnostic assessment.

Here we suggest appropriate formative feedback for a **Making Animals** activity:

Levels A - B	Provide stimulus material such as photographs of animals and plants. Ask them why these animals / plants are suited to these environments or even a more leading comment like 'Have you thought about...?'
Levels B - C	Try a **Mind Movie** to develop their idea of context. Ask what they see, hear, smell and then how they can use that information to design their animal. Ask 'If it needs X, what is needed to go with it?' eg, a tall animal would need strong legs.
Levels C - D	Encourage them to develop explanations for their choices. Ask questions: 'Will that characteristic be good enough in every situation that it is exposed to?'
Levels D - E	Ask them to speculate on a range of circumstances, for example whether their equatorial animal survives in both heavy rain and bright sun. This will allow them to test the validity of their choices. Ask them to explain their decisions to the class.
Levels E - F	These are high order thinkers. More penetrating debriefing, sharing and comparing ideas supports further progress.

Resource 9　　　**Assessment**

Levels of response	Indicators of Levels from pupils' work
Level A • Simple, general reasons are given but unrelated to context. • May include misconceptions and misinterpretations.	
Level B • Reasoning is related to context. • Context factors not clearly linked enough to suggest coherent understanding.	
Level C • Most choices are justified by context / place feature, which shows an overall appreciation of the situation in question. • Lack of specificity or evidence to reinforce justification.	
Level D • Some evidence to justify choices. • Reasoning may involve multiple factors and choices are both realistic and compatible.	
Level E • Generalisations begin to emerge about the choosing process. There is evidence of prioritising and choosing on the strength of need. • Students begin to draw upon own knowledge.	
Level F • Overall reasoning strategy with plenty of supporting detail. • Evidence of reappraisal of choices.	

Chapter 5

Five Ws

5 Five Ws (or what? where? who? when? why?)

Rationale

It is paradoxical that in many classrooms it is the people who know who ask the questions and those who don't who have to try and answer them. (see Dillon, 1988) However, NC geography KS3 is explicit in its requirement that

> 'In undertaking geographical enquiry, *pupils* should be taught to:
>
> a) ask geographical questions and...
>
> b) suggest appropriate sequences of investigation' (DfEE NC, 1999).

Progression in this skill is reflected in the Level descriptions and we should be supporting pupils to develop the skills of *independent* geographical enquiry. This is built on later, at GCSE, at AS and A Level where this vital skill is further developed in fieldwork and coursework activities.

Day to day classroom reality reflects a rather different situation in which teachers generally pose all the questions and their sequence and provide the relevant source material. It is tough to break away from this model of teaching.

5W is an approach that encourages pupils to ask questions and to consider the underlying logic of asking particular kinds of questions, in particular ways and in a particular order. It can help *pupils* in '*selecting* and using secondary sources of evidence' (NC A 2 d)) because pupils have to think about what they *need* to know and why they need to find it out before approaching the available resources. In other words, pupils gain some understanding and ownership of the process of geographical enquiry.

A major strength of the **5W** approach is the ease with which it can be transferred to other learning situations both in geography and across the curriculum such as in history, where the learner is challenged to make sense of and evaluate a variety of data. It is an 'advance organiser' for information and ideas for producing coherent, structured and detailed responses.

Consequently, **5W** is not *only* about questioning. In framing questions for themselves they are also considering the answers they are looking for. Pupils learn that the data they have access to may not necessarily answer all, or be relevant to, their questions. It must be intelligently sifted and evaluated. By contrast, many standard textbook activities need no more or less than what is provided on a double page spread. This encourages a culture of '*data dependency*' - a passive acceptance that the teacher will always provide exactly and *only* what the pupil needs. Through **5W** we try to encourage our pupils to sort through and to interrogate data, the sources of data and the reliability and adequacy of data. This is something that can be started in KS3 and should not suddenly be sprung on poor unsuspecting A Level students years later!

Your class may need to practise collaboration and group working. In this case, try using the **T-chart** *sounds like/looks like* activity under **launching** in *Exemplar 1*.

Enquiry is one of the generic NCTS as well as a specific requirement of NC geography.

Excellent discussion of the rationale of and implications for curriculum planning of the enquiry approach and ideas for implementation can be found in Davidson and Catling's Chapter *Towards the Question-led Curriculum 5-14*, in Fisher & Binns, 2000.

This connects well with NCTS Evaluation.

The San Francisco Earthquake 1989

Context

This example is based on a piece of work undertaken by Y9 pupils in the more able half of the year group of a large comprehensive. The 40 minute lesson formed part of a module on Tectonic Processes which was studied in the Spring Term. Pupils had already looked at where earthquakes happen and why they occur. The next step was to study the events and effects of an earthquake. When devised, the department happened to be well resourced with material about this particular earthquake but as new events come along and the 1989 earthquake recedes into history, it is easy to replace with another case study. The class was new to 5W.

Preparation

The main resource used was an article on the San Francisco earthquake of 1989 in *GeoActive No 26*. This publication was aimed at GCSE level but contained more detailed and contemporary information than our available textbooks. Pupils only needed help with a few terms, such as *CBD* and *Interstate*. Although the article itself contained most of the information needed for the subsequent task, additional data sources were accessible on the school library computers. In their own time, pupils could consult CD-ROMs such as *Violent Earth*, *Physical World* and *Encarta*.

Without the TT activity the resource could well have been too difficult for the pupils to use alone.

The class was arranged in friendship groups of between four and six pupils.

Launching

If your class has no track record of constructive and industrious collaboration (group working!) we would recommend a useful strategy called a '*T-chart*' or '*sounds like / looks like*' which can be a good starting point.

This is clearly a case of developing the Working with Others skill NCTS

This can be a small group or whole class activity. A large-scale version of the T-chart shown below is needed. Ask the pupils to imagine what a class that is working well in groups looks like and sounds like.

Looks like	Sounds like

Suggestions are then written in the chart. From these ideas the teacher then summarises what constitutes successful group work. You can then make it clear that these are the expectations for the following activity. The chart can be placed in a prominent position so that pupils and the teacher refer to it from time to time.

To introduce the 5W in such a way as to encourage all pupils to take part, we used a technique which we call '*think-pair-share*'. Pupils were given two minutes during which time they individually and silently thought of some questioning words, that is words in a sentence indicating that a question is being asked. After two minutes each pupil shared his/her words with another member of the group. Pairs then shared their words with the rest of the group. Finally, I asked for one word from each table and put them on the board. Five which are commonly used are WHAT? WHERE? WHO? WHEN? WHY? Depending on the choice of topic being studied it may be appropriate to include HOW? where a process is to be examined (on the grounds that like the other words it contains W and H!) and WHICH? when an element of decision-making is involved. We just call this 'geographers' licence'.

These are then confirmed to be appropriate words for questions to use in exploring an event or an issue. You can tell them that this is just like the board game '*Cluedo*' and the questions that need to be answered in order to solve the murder.

Although not the main objective of the lessons, planning, drafting and editing the report and selecting a style of writing to suit a particular audience was a strong feature of the second half of this lesson and follow-up. This is a prime example of how geography can be a vehicle for the development of literacy.

Instructions

1. Pupils were asked to imagine themselves to be newspaper reporters who have just been assigned to report on an earthquake that has hit the city of San Francisco.

2. On the plane across the Atlantic they must plan their research. To do this they were asked to draw a table of five columns, each headed with one of the **5Ws**. They were then asked to think of as many questions as they could that would best lead to an understanding of the disaster among the newspaper's readers. These were entered under the appropriate '**W**' heading. They could work individually, in pairs or as a group, but were only given about fifteen minutes to do this 'before the food and drink arrived and the in-flight movie began!'

3. After the allotted time, each table was asked to contribute one question and the class' ideas were then summarised on the board. This gave less able pupils the chance to benefit from other ideas and add to their own. Of course there was some repetition and similarity of questions but initially pupils were told to consider them to be all of equal merit. Examples:

   > *When did it happen? What was the damage? Who was affected? Where did most of it happen? Who are the 'heroes'? When might it happen again? Who pays for the damage? What are the emergency services like? How did people feel when it happened? What did they do? What caused it? Why did some buildings stay up while others fell down? Why does anyone live somewhere so dangerous? What miraculous escapes were there?*

4. Groups were asked to number their questions into what seemed to them to be a logical order. They were free to discard any that they did not now think worthwhile asking. Their ordering was to be subject to revision later. Remember though – pupils knew very little as yet about this particular earthquake without the benefit of the *GeoActive* article. Minds were focused on what information would be needed for their newspaper report.

5. The lesson was straightforward from now on. I gave out the *GeoActive* article which pupils studied to find answers to as many of their questions as possible.

6. After about 10 minutes I asked if they had any questions that couldn't be answered from the resource and asked if they could think of other ways to find out. These included textbooks, library books, CD-ROM and Internet research and newspaper or TV reports. I told them that further research was their homework and that I would show a news video at the start of the next lesson. (In hindsight, this would have been more effective and motivating if I'd shown it during the second half of the lessons)

7. With 15 minutes to go, I set them the task of drafting their reports, recognising that they'd need to add bits later and perhaps reorganise their reports.

Managing the activity

Circulating between the groups helped me monitor progress and offer support where it was needed. Sometimes this was to provoke thinking about what kind of *answer* might be given in response to a question. Sometimes to reduce the vagueness of a question such as *'What effects has the earthquake had?'* I simply asked *'On what or whom?'*

While collating sample questions on the board I noticed that there were fields of information that the questions were not reaching. I tried to elicit some by asking *'Does anyone think it would help if we knew something about…?'* and then invite them to phrase an appropriate question.

Some needed help with the resource whilst others completed this section unaided. It was important to check that they were including sufficient detail. I stressed that the editors would not accept something vague and general - the public needed to be informed of what had happened and why.

Sometimes groups try to order their questions under each **W** heading. This is *not helpful* as the columns contain a mixture of question types. Verbal disputes do occasionally break out and you must be on hand to mediate.

Less able pupils might need some support in the writing up, perhaps through the use of a writing frame to help them set out their report.

Sharing thinking is a particular strength of TT activities. Everyone, including the teacher, can benefit from others' ideas. It is sometimes called 'Distributed Cognition'.

This process is at the heart of Enquiry. They have prepared an 'advanced organiser'.

This is an instant formative response.

Sheila King refers to 'big questions' and 'little questions' (*Teaching Geography*, vol 24,1999). This is well worth reading.

The report writing phase was quite a challenge. Groups had to discuss their ideas for the structure of their reports and it was by no means certain that they saw themselves as reporters for the same kind of newspaper! Moreover, those who read the back pages of newspapers first were familiar with the style peculiar to sports reporters which leads a match report with an account of a hotly disputed penalty midway through the second half. It can be several column inches later that the reader finds out what happened in the first half. It is not hard to imagine some national newspapers reporting an earthquake story in a similar vein by focusing first on the remarkable survival of a pet hamster miraculously saved from oblivion by the structural strength of its wheel. We left the choice of the style of writing for a particular audience to the pupils, but you could be more specific if you wanted.

Debriefing

I asked pupils three questions:

Firstly, *'How did you construct your questions?'*
   Most responses echoed these themes:
   - We thought about the information that readers would want to know and made up questions which would help us find this out;
   - We made sure that the questions would give us clear answers about the earthquake. You (the teacher!) made us think about the answers you might get as well as the question.

Secondly, *'How did you decide that a question was important enough to include?'*
   - We checked to see if the question related to the information we needed;
   - We chose the questions that would give us most information about the earthquake and those that would pull information together;
   - We chose questions that would give us good, detailed answers.

Thirdly, *'What makes a good question?'* They suggested the following:
   - One that needs more than a one word answer, like an explanation;
   - A good question is clear, well structured and makes sense;
   - One which provides a good, detailed and informative answer;
   - One that is open to lots of answers.

We spotted a tension between the first and last points here which provided an excellent opportunity to introduce the concept of open and closed questions of which there was an ample supply of both. In discussion they could also recognise categories of likely answers, some of which had been introduced while doing other thinking skills activities, for example **Fact or Opinion** and *'trigger and background'* factors to events in **Mysteries**.

They were also asked to think about other instances in geography and other subjects, where they could use the **5W**'s technique. Some ideas were:

   - Finding out about a volcanic eruption, flood or famine; (They tend to have a penchant for catastrophes!)
   - When you are starting a project;
   - In history, when you have to find out what happened or decide if something like a document is accurate or true;
   - In science when you have to develop your own experiment.

It was pleasing that the class could identify this technique as not only transferable between subjects but also in other geographical contexts. The class actually suggested using **5W** on several subsequent occasions.

Assessment

We find that for KS3 pupils, **5W** activities are valuable sources of evidence for pupils' Levels of attainment. Firstly you have a written record of what pupils consider being valuable geographical questions and secondly the written outcomes display the levels of understanding of the subject content and the inter-relationship of its component parts. Lower Level responses tend simply to 'tell the story' of the earthquake whilst pupils operating at higher Levels are able to link causes and effects, explain processes and begin

This is a reminder of the major contribution that geography can make to the literacy agenda.

This is real differentiation by outcome.

This anticipation of the appropriateness of different information for different interested parties is another exercise in classification.

This episode shows pupils confidently talking about thinking processes. They are using metacognition.

This might have been a good point to ask pupils if they could recognise cues in the teacher's questioning to the kinds of responses required.

5W is a powerful and flexible heuristic - a general problem solving strategy. The range of answers shows its flexibility.

Historical enquiry at KS3 and source working in general involve essentially the same cognitive processes.

to make value judgements about human responses to the earthquake. In this instance, pupils were not asked in their written work to make references to any other earthquakes, make predictions or assess its wider significance in order to achieve the highest Levels, but with a little modification, the activity could be structured to allow this.

There was no upper limit to the quantity or quality of questions they were able to generate. The order in which they decided to tackle them was also interesting in that most pupils chose *not* to ask all their questions with the same **W** at the same time but instead organised them to pursue particular lines of enquiry, for example: Where was the worst damage? What kind of damage was done? Why were some buildings affected worse than others? Who checks how they are built? What precautions are being taken to prevent the same thing happening again? I have been surprised and impressed by how well pupils have got the hang of this. *TTG* seems to do that a lot!

Self-assessment
Pupils can be encouraged to reflect on the pre-writing stage by asking them to record which of their original questions they had rejected and why. Later they can consider which questions had proved to be meaningful, though to some extent this is dependent upon the variety and quality of the resources at the pupils' disposal. You can also ask if the order in which they posed their questions was logical to them.

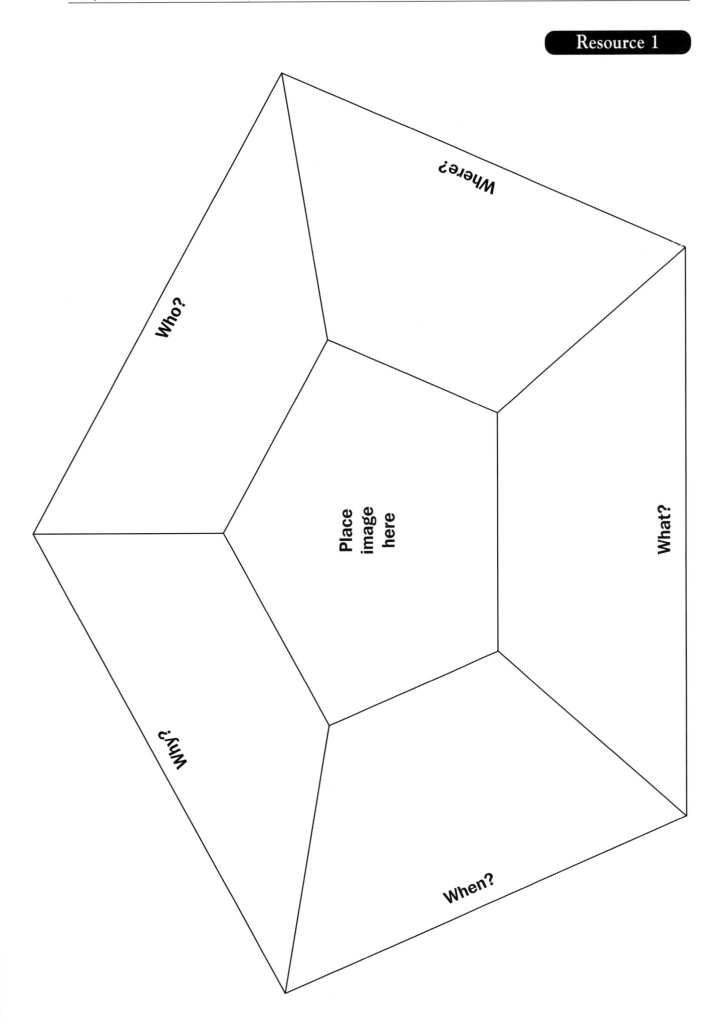

Farming in Upland Areas

Context

This Exemplar was used as a revision exercise with average and above average ability Y11 GCSE pupils as a means of interrogating a photograph of an upland landscape. They had already covered the sections of the syllabus that included Glaciation, National Parks, Upland Farming in Britain, Population and Settlement, and Transport. This activity served to integrate knowledge and understanding of these topics in one locational context and to encourage pupils to explore the ways in which the topics impinge on each other.

> Exploring a range of geographical concepts in one case study makes this a potential candidate for a **Concept Map**!

It is all too easy for us to focus pupils' attention on textual data at the expense of exploiting photographic resources for their geographical meaning. (see **Reading Photographs** *TTG p135*) The activities in some textbooks make poor use of images that appear as decorative illustrations rather than as thought provoking resources. We use **5W** as a way of encouraging pupils to look analytically at images.

Preparation

A slide of a North Pennine valley was selected (Uswayford, Northumberland) and an outline sketch (*Resource 2*) of the scene (*Resource 3*) was drawn from the slide by projecting it onto a sheet of A3 paper pinned to a wall. The landscape features were outlined with a thick black marker pen. (This technique masks my inability to draw decent field sketches!) This drawing was then reduced to fit the centre of *Resource 1*. I then printed enough copies for each member of the class. I also prepared OHTs of *Resource 2* and of *Resource 4* and set up the OHP.

At the start of the lesson I gave these out, one each, and some lined paper for drafting questions on.

Launching

I explained the reason for this activity by telling them that their ability to ask appropriate questions by themselves and then to find answers to them would have a direct benefit to their geographical investigation (GCSE Independent Enquiry) as well as the quality of their answers to examination questions.

> An example of connecting to very instrumental contexts.

I reminded the class that photographs often appeared in examination papers and they would need some practice in interpreting them for geographical meaning. To do this they would need to not only look at the image as a whole but also to unpick its components, both physical and human. Asking questions of the landscape would help to understand it. The class also has previous experience of being asked to consider the 'bigger picture', that is, what lies outside the frame and behind the photographer and how representative or typical they think the image might be of the rest of the landscape. (Using a range of photos is also an option).

On this occasion I asked them to work in pairs but to work on their own sketch outline. The projector (aimed at the A3 paper on the side wall) was switched on and the blinds were then closed.

Instructions

> The ability to describe is improved over time by growing understanding of the term 'characteristic' and the use of several characteristics to describe.

1 I asked the class to study closely the picture on the screen and annotate the features of the landscape in as much detail as possible such as 'stone farmhouse' and 'big, leafy trees' rather than simply 'buildings' and 'trees'. They were told to put their notes in the margin around the sketch.

2 I then asked them to work in pairs to write **5W** questions that, when answered, would allow the pupils to demonstrate as much relevant knowledge and understanding as possible about the North Pennine landscape. The aim was to find out more about the things they had annotated around the picture. (You might need to half open a curtain or blind at this point!)

3 The next step was to evaluate the questions that they had written down. I gave them 10 minutes to discuss their own and neighbouring pairs' questions. I showed the OHT of *Resource 4* as an aid to evaluating them.

4   I then asked them to try and classify their own questions by labelling them A,B,C or D:

    A   those leading to brief factual answers that were interesting but not 'helpful';

    B   those leading to brief factual answers that were 'helpful';

    C   those needing extended explanations;

    D   those needing references to particular places, people, processes or things.

5   I asked for examples of each category and whether each kind would be worth asking 'if we wanted to understand the geography in the photograph' (KS3 pupils don't have much idea of the breadth of the subject whereas by Y11 they know that almost anything can be!) This took about 7 minutes and some were already thinking in terms of coursework titles such as 'Would this make a suitable site for a caravan park?' which wasn't quite what I had in mind at the time!

6   Pupils were given the opportunity to write/rewrite appropriate questions.

7   I then gave the pairs 5 minutes to try and sort the questions into an order so that those that were asking something about the same theme would be grouped together then organised into a logical sequence.

Managing the activity

Step 3 above was interesting. Two pairs were reluctant to cross out or change any of their questions. I think they felt that they had 'done the job' and were reluctant to 'undo' any of it. Maybe my questioning wasn't clear enough or over-sophisticated. I found that if I pointed to individual questions and asked them to say *why* they wanted to know about it, they began to reword and cross some out which left them a little short of questions. I had to give them the opportunity to take another look at the slide by leaving the projector on for them to generate some new ones. It was noticeable that the other pairs looked back at the screen from time to time too.

> This observation is an example of diagnostic assessment and subsequent scaffolding.

Debriefing

The final stage of the lesson was used to emphasise the value of the activity by asking questions such as: -

1   *'What do you think the purpose of this activity might be?'*

2   *'Why should you ask yourself questions?'*

3   *'Why do you need to be aware of the range of questions that could be asked?'*

Someone muttered that he couldn't see the point if the same picture didn't come up in the exam but he was sorted out by his partner who pointed out that he couldn't remember ever seeing a picture he knew exactly in exams but he'd now got an idea of what to do with *any* picture. *'It'll give you something to write about'*.

> A model for interrogating a photograph is being generated and increases the chances of transfer.

The second question drew this comment: *'If you're asking yourself questions, you've got to try and answer them as well which is hard. You might not know. You have to think really hard to find it'*.

> Asking oneself questions is part of the process of developing inner speech, a feature of metacognitive processes.

The third question led to a short discussion of what in the end amounted to an understanding of open and closed questions: those that need you to 'say a lot, to say why things happen' (type C above) and those that need 'simple answers. Sometimes one word will do.' (types B & D above) Sadly we didn't have enough time to talk around which might be the more useful. However, this agenda was pursued in subsequent lessons.

Follow-up

Pupils were asked to try to answer their questions using their own exercise book notes, revision guides, text books and other sources in the classroom such as National Park leaflets on farming as a homework/revision exercise.

> **5W** has provided a very useful structure to support writing in this Exemplar.

Resource 2

Uswayford Farm, Nothumberland

Resource 3

Uswayford Farm, Nothumberland

Questions About Questions!

- Would this question provide us with the kind of answer to help us understand something? (eg, a question of little value might be about the name of a person in a picture)

- Will there be a definite answer (closed question) or a speculative one (open question)?

- Might the answer make us want to ask another (especially 'why?') question?

- Will the question need a fact, description, explanation or speculation?

- Does the question focus on causes or effects?

- Has your neighbour got a better question about...?

- Have we studied anything else that might relate to the question?

Any questions?

Exemplar 3

Natural Environments

Context

Our Y9 Natural Environments unit of work introduces pupils to a range of contrasting environments and how humans interact with them. The National Curriculum (NC KS3 6e) specifies as a minimum entitlement that one major biome should be studied. Over a total of three lessons, pupils would study one of their own and become acquainted with others as presented by other groups. Given this time span of involvement, only the initial **5W** part is described. In this average ability Y9 class of 27, pupils have already had some experience of **5W** in other contexts such as *Exemplar 1*.

However, I had another objective in mind. Some pupils were not the most cooperative of workers in groups. I even had to abandon a group work lesson some months previously. As a way of raising their consciousness about the way they work and to recognise their responsibility to the group, I decide to re-run 'looks like, sounds like' as described in *Exemplar 1* and to include a self-assessment of their contribution to the process (see *Resource 5*). You can use this after any phase of group working or you may prefer to leave it until the very end of the unit.

This is an ideal way of contributing to the Key Skills: Improving Own Learning and Performance.

Preparation

I printed enough copies of *Resource 6* enlarged onto A3 paper, one for each group, (You can easily customise this to suit your own needs) and a self-evaluation slip (*Resource 5*) for each person.

You need quite a lot of resources about natural environments to be available at the same time for different groups to work on, but I think it's worth the hassle, so over break I made clusters of resource materials for each environment plus a 'reference section' of generic sources such as wildlife books from the school library and atlases. I also loaded *Encarta* onto the one PC available.

I employed a couple of early birds to arrange the chairs so that groups of about 4 could work together around tables. Friendship groupings had not been too successful last time so I numbered them 1-7 in order as they entered the room then allocated each number to a different 'base'.

Launching

This year group likes wildlife programmes on TV so I asked them to name some of the wild animals they had seen programmes about. This yielded an interesting selection from tree frogs to coyotes. I asked them to imagine what it might be like to live in the same sort of place (I decided not to take the opportunity to use **Mind Movies** in the interests of speed) and most responses were along the lines of 'nice to visit but not to live' for a variety of reasons: dangers, heat, cold among others. I pointed out that some people do live in such environments but often not as comfortably or in the same ways as we do. This seemed to be a sufficient hook for me to explain that we would investigate a range of contrasting environments between us but that each group would become 'experts' about one in particular. If they could devise good **5W** questions, they would find things out that the other groups wouldn't know. (This element of one-upmanship seemed to appeal!)

I told them that, as experts, they would have the chance to share what they have found out with the others (OK, it's a bit of a con, but I prefer this kind of phrasing to 'you are going to have to...' which always makes tasks seem so burdensome!) I also said that the most successful teams would be the ones that worked best together with contributions from everyone.

After the 'looks like, sounds like' introduction, little additional advice was needed as pupils were already familiar with the questioning words. If your group is new to this activity you might like to proceed as suggested in *Exemplar 1* first.

Instructions

1 I first ran 'looks like - sounds like' as in *Exemplar 1*.

2 Allocate a different natural environment to investigate by lucky dip to each group. I put the names of the environments on slips of paper for groups to pick one out of a biscuit tin. These were: hot desert; equatorial rain forest; high mountains;

coniferous forest; tundra; savanna; and temperate grassland. You may prefer another way of doing this if you think you can prevent the inevitable groans about one being 'harder' than another! (The grasslands didn't go down too well) You could reduce the variety by making groups larger though that holds inherent risks, or double up on some environments.

3   I gave out *Resource 6* to each group and gave them 15 minutes to devise at least one kind of **5W** question for each box.

4   Once each sheet was completed, they were redistributed and allocated to a different group so that they could study the questions on a different ecosystem. Time was allowed for each group to read through the questions and discuss possible improvements, which were then added in pencil.

5   The sheets were then returned to their owners who had a couple of minutes to decide how to respond to the suggestions of their peers, if at all.

> Feedback here is being provided by peer assessment.

Managing the activity

I only needed to intervene when anyone went off-task but they generally just needed to be reminded that everyone should make a contribution. Having mixed the groups though, some gelled better than others. I went round each group to monitor progress and, much as in managing *Exemplar 1*, reminded them of their own previous conclusions about the characteristics of questions such as those that are open and closed questions. Quick workers were encouraged to develop further questions in each category.

When sheets had been passed on there were some comments about how similar many of the questions were and I made a point of complimenting them on getting the hang of asking geographical questions. I could also hear some groups identifying some they could use themselves.

I had not anticipated that where one group had suggested a modification to a question, there would need to be an opportunity for them to discuss why. For instance, the question *'What weather do they have there?'* had been altered to *What climate do they have there?* In fact the originators had wanted to know if their region had hurricanes and tornados and the short exchange between the two groups certainly helped clarify the distinction between the terms and led to extra questions being scribbled down by other groups! I would build in this inter-group discussion stage more formally next time. I think all the groups can benefit from hearing or participating in it.

> A further example of feedback which relates to Key Skills: Working with Others.

I gave them five minutes to decide who would research which questions before carrying out the group work questionnaire *(Resource 5)*.

Debriefing

I asked them if they thought the team had come up with a better selection of questions than they could have done on their own and they nearly all agreed. One of the more able girls thought she would have done, but having had to defend some of her own questions and to argue for and against others, she felt more confident that she knew that she had 'got the idea'.

> Debriefing helps build insight which contributes to Key Skills: Improving Own Learning and Performance.

I reminded them of the teamwork objective not only for the unit as a whole but for the **5W** stage and referred them to *Resource 5*. I said they could do this privately and stick it in their books but would be asked to look at it again at the start of the next lesson. I was pleased that most took this moment of reflection seriously though I got the impression (perhaps fairly) that they might have done better in a different group.

Follow-up

The task for the next few lessons was research - based, making use of the library, class texts, CD-ROMs, photo packs, geographical magazines and (over lunchtimes) the Internet. The task for each group was to find answers to their questions and plan and produce a short presentation on their particular environment. Each lesson ended with a few minutes when pupils were asked to comment on how their research was progressing. We discussed if some types of questions were easier to research than others, which were proving to be the most useful resources, and anything unexpected that they had unearthed. (For example, the Siberian meteorite crater generated a bit of distracting interest!) They were also asked to consider the specific study skills they were developing and how these could be applied elsewhere.

> This highlights how metacognition can grow over time.

Most of the final presentations displayed a lot more individual enthusiasm than usual and the real problem was to keep them down to reasonable lengths. There was a lot of information about animal life but less about vegetation and the links between the two. Next time I might restrict them to reference to just two creatures that are adapted to the environment in different ways. One group had not really been switched on by its environment and the result was a somewhat monotonous string of facts. Not surprisingly, the less able in the group chose to read from prepared scripts.

Assessment

Some colleagues may think that evaluating group work is outside the remit of the geography department, but in fact it is a very important life-long skill for pupils to develop and we cannot pretend that it cannot be done. It is a significant part of NC English up to KS4.

KS3/4 English

En 1: Speaking and Listening

Group discussion and interaction:

3. *To participate effectively as members of different groups, pupils should be taught to:*

a) *make different types of contributions to groups, adapting their speech to their listeners and the activity;*

b) *take different views into account and modify their own views in the light of what others say;*

c) *sift, summarise and use the most important points;*

d) *take different roles in the organisation, planning and sustaining of groups;*

e) *help the group to complete its tasks by varying contributions appropriately, clarifying and synthesising others' ideas, taking them forward and building on them to reach conclusions, negotiating consensus or agreeing to differ.*

(DfEE NC, 1999, p46)

Transferable skills as with spelling, grammar and writing for different audiences must not be left to the English department alone. The development of transferable skills is what *Thinking Through Geography* is all about.

The final presentations were joint efforts and groups had freedom to choose their means of presentation. Only practicalities prevented one group from putting together a Powerpoint presentation but most others opted for poster presentations. The unit of work also included an element of peer evaluation. We find that pupils can be highly critical as well as complimentary with each other about their work and we have to remind them to be sensitive to their colleagues' efforts. Over time, we feel that peer and self-assessment helps undermine the notion that work is only done in order to please the teacher.

> Differentiation by outcome allows pupils to express their understanding in ways that they find comfortable. There is an almost obsessional demand for evidence of achievement to be in written form in some classrooms but it is no more reliable as a measure of achievement that, say, oral evidence. In both cases they represent pupils' knowledge and understanding at the time of writing or speaking only.

At the end of the unit (3 lessons), groups were asked to evaluate their own presentations and make suggestions about ways in which they could have been improved. Many bemoaned the difficulty of finding information for some answers or sources that went way over their heads (eg, some Internet sources). Some admitted to changing some of their questions to fit what they found of interest and relevance. Now, I'm still thinking about this! If police investigators came across evidence that they hadn't originally thought of looking for, would they ignore it?

More than one group criticised one of its members for not pulling his weight: an interesting application of peer pressure on the anti-effort culture that sometimes affects this class!

Afterthoughts

I have used **5W** with a number of classes with a range of ages and abilities. Sometimes I have used it as a stimulus for the start of a lesson, especially with a photograph or an artefact. On other occasions **5W** has been the major feature of the lesson. Not all pupils see the point of this activity straight away. Far from being lazy, they just want to 'get on with the job' and would prefer to be given the questions needed to guide them directly to the necessary information. Over the years this is what many pupils have come to expect. **5W** helps them to actively be geographers.

GCSE pupils are required to design and conduct their own Enquiries which in most cases involves both primary and secondary data collection. In anticipation of this we have added a stage to the **5W** process when used with examination classes by asking them to consider what the sources of data might be for the answers to their questions. There is no reason why this should not form a part of every **5W**. In *Exemplar 1*, Y9 pupils act as imaginary journalists and I'm sure they could have worked out which data they would need from site visits, interviews with the public, emergency services and city officials, consulting public records, geological maps, scientific experts and so on.

Less able pupils find generating questions difficult. Initially their suggestions may lack a geographical focus. They are often closed and people-centred, but they do get better, so do not give up. They can be helped by ensuring that the topic for the questions is tightly defined eg, 'The effects of the San Francisco earthquake' as opposed to a vague 'Report on the San Francisco earthquake' which invites a 'write anything and everything you can about...'

In our examination classes I am sure that learning to develop good questioning techniques helps them to better understand what the examiner expects. A natural extension to **5W** for GCSE and A Level students is for pupils to structure their own questions using key command words from past papers as stimuli. An understanding of the functions of these commands is essential for candidates to gain maximum credit for their geographical knowledge and understanding. Such is the versatility of this simple thinking skill activity.

I am not aware yet of any pupils calculating that asking 'difficult' questions is making a rod for their own back or that more questions mean more to answer. These are collaborative ventures so the weight is not carried on one set of shoulders. The generally positive attitude to the exercise is that they feel that they are answering their questions, not the teacher's.

> 'Motivation and engagement' is one of the themes of the TTL programme. Pupils need to be given this to become a reality.

5W is a simple yet effective approach which enables pupils to develop an enquiry approach to their own research. In the process, they are learning how different kinds of questions elicit different kinds of responses, reading for meaning and writing with a purposeful focus. It counters the tendency of many pupils to find all they can about a topic and churn it out indiscriminately. (Internet sources are a particular pain in this regard!) We feel that there are benefits in relation to GCSE examination questions, most of which are structured to a common formula that starts with easy data retrieval tasks. These provide context for subsequent increasingly challenging questions that require analysis and explanation. Pupils seem to have a clearer idea of what kinds of responses are needed for the different kinds of questions as indicated by the command words.

> There are strong elements of planning, drafting, revising, editing, publishing, collectively known as the writing process (Wray & Lewis, 1997)

Resource 5   **Group Work Questionnaire**

Date:

Name:

Put a tick in the right hand column in a position between left and right to indicate how much you agree or disagree with the statement

Statement	Strongly Disagree Strongly Agree
I enjoyed working in this group	
We used our time to good effect	
We organised ourselves well	
We were imaginative in our approach	
We were all involved in the tasks	
We were interested in the tasks	
I listened to what others had to say	
The others listened to what I had to say	
I had things to say but didn't say them	
The group had more ideas that I had on my own	
We were all involved in reaching decisions	
Differences of opinion were resolved sensibly.	
I had influence on the decisions	
There were ways in which I hindered the work of the group	
The group was dominated by some members	
The end results were good	

I could have helped the group more if...

The group would have worked better if...

Next time I am involved in group activities I will...

I will also...

PLACE

Locating this environment

CLIMATE

The seasonal pattern of weather conditions

LANDSCAPES

The shape and surface features of the land

FLORA

Plant life

FAUNA

Animal life

FOOD

HUMAN FEATURES

Noticeable things made by people

WATER

In this environment

Resource 6

SETTLEMENT
Living in this environment

TRANSPORT
Getting about in this environment

SOCIAL LIVES
Quality of life and customs

ECONOMY
Making a living

ENVIRONMENTAL IMPACT
Effects of human activity

SAFETY
Dangers of living here

FREE CHOICE
Something else you'd like to know about

FREE CHOICE
Something else you'd like to know about

Chapter 6

Taboo

6 Taboo

Rationale

Talk is the natural medium through which meaning is clarified.

Taboo is a game played in many homes and is sometimes seen in TV game shows. The beauty of it, organised as a team game as we describe, is that pupils really get engaged in thinking collaboratively within a context of friendly competition. The essence of many successful and enduring games is that they **do** provide sufficient intellectual challenge for the players. You soon get bored with those that don't. Consider the deductive reasoning in *Cluedo* and the calculation of chance and speculative investment strategies of *Monopoly*. **Taboo** is challenging yet simplicity itself to set up and is fun for all the family (ie, a range of ages and abilities).

Taboo is a game involving describing given words without being able to use those which most naturally come to mind. If you are not familiar with it, imagine trying to describe a pizza without being able to use these words: round, flat, tomato, cheese, dough or Italy. Now consider what is involved in describing 'evaporation' without using words such as water, vapour, heat or gas. It may seem perverse to discourage the use of words you might **wish** pupils to use in their descriptions and explanations so is there any 'method in this madness'?

This exemplifies that examination success is as much in the minds of TT teachers as anyone else's. TT is not a sideline activity. It is an important strategy for raising achievement.

In a recent GCSE examination paper at Foundation Level the command words 'describe' and 'explain' appeared 19 times. In the higher tier paper they occurred no less than 33 times. These are clearly skills of fundamental importance. Although candidates were only asked to provide definitions twice there were plenty of opportunities to make use of proper geographical terminology in their answers. Experience tells us that pupils frequently make a hash of definitions, descriptions and explanations even if they have been clearly recorded in their exercise books. They may also lack confidence in using appropriate language for the subject.

Taboo has the advantage of not being dependent upon high levels of literacy and is therefore accessible to the poorer readers who none-the-less may have good oral ability. Pupils have to think and talk about the *meaning* of the word and in doing so, construct and clarify deeper conceptual understanding of geographical terminology. They become more competent at describing and explaining in geographical language with confidence.

As well as serving a geographical purpose, it is easy to see how **Taboo** encourages **literacy development**. The National Literacy Strategy describes the literate pupil as having an interest in words and their meanings and a growing vocabulary. One of its word level objectives at KS3 is 'to use alternate words and expressions which are more accurate and interesting than the common choices'. At sentence level we find that pupils should 'discuss, proof-read and edit their own writing for clarity and correctness' (NLS, 2000). **Taboo** is therefore a strong contributor to these objectives.

Taboo provides the teacher and the pupil with feedback and the key to effective use of assessment. See Black & Wiliam, 1998 and Hay McBer to DfEE, 2000.

Taboo can be a powerful tool for **diagnostic** assessment. Where pupils have to decide on their own taboo words (as they do in *Exemplar 2*) the teacher can readily see the differences in pupils' understanding from the length and composition of their initial lists of taboo words. Moreover, it is quite easy to spot misconception and confusion.

So it serves a **formative** role too. It lets the teacher know where they have been ineffective. If an explanation has been rushed or poorly planned, you can be sure it will show up in this activity and you know what you have to revisit or approach again differently.

I find that the pupils who do not work well in groups or pairs tend not to choose the best taboo words so through debriefing you can highlight the importance of discussion which of course involves using speaking and listening skills.

See also article by Norton, Hundy & Adams: Teaching Geography Vol. 23/4 October 1998

So, is there 'method in this madness' after all? I think there is if it encourages pupils to:
- define key geographical terms;
- use prior knowledge and understanding;
- employ parallels and analogies;
- demonstrate knowledge of case studies;
- develop a more extensive vocabulary;
- make connections with the world *they* live in (rather than ours);
- participate in a fun activity and gain self-confidence at the same time;
- improve their responses to those 33 command words...

The Water Cycle

Context

Here we have a standard Key Stage 3 topic (Y8 in our case) where, on occasions, the hard-pressed teacher is tempted to whiz through an explanation then tell pupils to copy the diagram, label it from the book and learn it for homework. Many pupils can do this with all the technical words in the 'correct' places but we were unhappy with this. We found that many pupils genuinely believed that all precipitation falls on the hills and secondly that they were memorising the words and their relative locations on the diagram with little if any understanding of *how* the processes involved such as evapo-transpiration actually work, even though they had encountered the term in science. In other words they were memorising the diagram and its labels without fully understanding what they represented. (A good way to test this is to draw a diagram with a different orientation, without arrows and boxes for the words and set them the usual task).

There are many pupil misconceptions about the processes involved in clouds and precipitation, some of them unfortunately introduced by teachers.

A second reason for using **Taboo** was to introduce an easy strategy to colleagues new to thinking skills. Although trialled in a 50 minute lesson with a top set in Y8, it worked very well with only minor changes across the full ability range including as a refresher exercise for a GCSE class.

Another example of a *TTG* strategy being used in a 'goal orientated' way.

This may seem obvious but it does help if pupils have encountered the concepts in the topic before they play the game!

Preparation

Taboo in this format presents few management issues but several things should be considered in advance:

- Check that the terms used on the **Taboo** cards are appropriate to the way you have taught the topic. We chose only those that we have used in our teaching. You can easily make others for *surface run-off* or *infiltration* if you wish and substitute any you do not want to use.

- Group composition: this is an activity where pupils clarify meaning through discussion so you may wish to differentiate by mixing abilities. Alternatively you may wish to let them choose for themselves and give less able groups 'easier' words (concepts) to work with. Three per group is ideal and any more than four usually results in someone taking a back seat.

- The more professional looking the cards the better. I printed onto coloured card, covered it with clear sticky-backed laminate then guillotined it. The cards last longer this way. *(Resource 1)*

- Decide how to organise feedback of definitions to the class and how to score the teams *(see later)*.

- Put all textbooks, exercise books and files away. This is generally a popular instruction.

- Provide plenty of scrap paper for each group.

- Make sure you have a master copy of the words on the card for adjudication purposes.

Launching

As with all group activities, interest has to be engaged to stimulate the participation of the whole class. Applying the principle of relating the activity to the pupils' interests and experiences, the inaugural launch went thus:

Teacher: *How many of you like eating pizza?* (Nods and salivation all round) *With a partner, jot down the six best words you would use to describe a pizza to someone who had never seen one before (but by happy coincidence also speaks English).*

(2 minutes later) Hands up if you used 'cheese'?, 'tomato'?, "Italy'?, 'salami'?, 'round'? 'flat'?

*Now think of words and phrases you might use to describe a pizza if you are **not allowed** to use these obvious words.*

If you've seen 'They Think It's All Over' on TV (after the 9pm watershed!) you will know the game at the end when team members have to guess the sportsperson on the card from someone's

Replicating formats of activities with which pupils have familiarity and positive attitudes is immensely motivational. There can be few teachers in the country who have not offered a pupil the chance to 'ask the audience' or 'phone a friend'!

description. This activity is like that but with words on the card you are forbidden to use, like describing David Beckham without mentioning Posh or football.

After a couple of minutes the alternative ways of describing a pizza can be shared.

Instructions

1 Divide the class into nine groups as there are nine cards and make sure each one has enough paper for preparing their descriptions and another piece of paper for recording the words of the other groups that they identify. Give each group a letter or number.

2 Tell the class that each group will be given a card with a term at the top that is something to do with the water cycle and a list of words below. They are going to have to describe or explain it but it is forbidden to use **any** of the words on the card or variations of them.

3 Give them about five minutes to plan a description / explanation of the key term that they will later present to the other groups that will try and identify it.

4 Elect a spokesperson or agree to share the task of presenting the group's agreed description.

5 Explain the scoring system to prevent groups conjuring up inaccurate or bizarre descriptions to deliberately stop the other groups from identifying the key word! (Yes, they do try this on!) I suggest:

> Scoring: 1 point to each of the other groups that correctly identifies the description.
>
> 1 point to the describing team for each of the others that gets the right answer.
>
> If you hear a *taboo* word in use you might wish to cancel the points for that card.

6 Give about five minutes for all groups to discuss and agree the descriptions for their key term.

7 Ask each group's spokesperson in turn slowly to read out their descriptions twice, allowing time for groups to confer and record each key term they can identify.

Managing the activity

Pupils can sometimes circumvent the challenge in the game by using ideas from elsewhere in their curriculum such as using H2O when 'water' is *taboo* or simply translations into a foreign language. While we would generally encourage such strategies in other circumstances they have to be banned in this one!

The ability to challenge and support groups is critical and can be developed over time.

Groups that are quick to finish may be challenged to make their descriptions more concise, more comprehensive or to redraft it to 'make it more geographical'. Strugglers can be supported by asking them to talk you through their understanding of the key term such as *'What actually is water vapour, then?'* You may need to prompt their memories of a case study, a story or a diagram that you have used in class. Lots of positive reinforcement is useful at this stage for all groups.

Feedback can be almost instantaneous in the debriefing and all the more effective by occurring while the pupils' thinking is still 'warm'.

Eavesdrop but try not to intervene in their discussions unless they have gone completely off track. This way much can be learned about the security of their understanding and how collectively they are able to construct meaning throughout the group. Listening can also provide you with some valuable overheard phrases which should be jotted down for use in debriefing.

Finally each group should have 9 key words written down. You can decide how to score but I find it easy to identify which teams to award points to if there is a nominated person per group who puts up a hand when their team correctly identified the key word from the description read out by each of the other groups.

Debriefing

This was rather more prescriptive than I would usually be because I designed this Exemplar for beginners and non-specialists.

When I first use **Taboo** with a new class, I usually start by saying *'Normally I'd be expecting* *you to use the best vocabulary you possibly can to describe or explain something. So, what's the point of this game?'* Apart from the odd one that believes it is my job to make life difficult, they usually say it makes them think and discuss what something means. That's enough for me!

In this lesson we then discussed why the winning group won. Apart from shouts of 'cheating', they said they could identify (remember) the key words from the descriptions, so it was a compliment to everyone that they had been accurate and inventive enough!

Pupils were asked to individually write down their responses to the following questions. I find that this makes it less likely that the lazier pupils will switch off and leave the 'hard bit' to others!

- How did this activity make you think?
- What did you have to do to be 'successful'?
- What are the features of a 'good' explanation?

We then discussed them.

> Allowing all pupils to think before the discussion means that more pupils will be prepared to contribute.

The activity made them think hard about different ways to describe things and to talk with the group about the meaning of the key words. Some found using examples helped, especially those I had used in my explanations in previous lessons. (Reassuring evidence that they'd been listening!) We agreed that these would be valuable to include in exam answers. Someone pointed out that if you didn't know much about the key word, you might not be able to describe it even by using all the *taboo* words anyway. So, we concluded that the best explanations and descriptions had come from the words that were understood the best.

They felt that some words were 'easier' than others to work with. This is an interesting point to think about. While some terms are short or in every day use and easy to remember the concept itself may be complex. 'Condensation' is arguably no more difficult to read or understand than 'transpiration', but pupils usually get the one before the other because their breadth and depth of understanding of 'condensation' are greater.

> Generally, the more **Taboo** words pupils generate, the better their understanding of the concept or process.

When using **Taboo** again with a group it is worthwhile refreshing their memories of this discussion before the activity begins. If you use variants described in the following two Exemplars, debriefing can be developed further.

Follow-up

I set them the task of using the words in their own explanation combined with the words on the **Taboo** card to produce a 'best' explanation of the key word. This was to incorporate the characteristics of a good explanation that had been distilled from debriefing. There was a strong sense of ownership of these definitions. If you run out of time this can be a homework activity instead, but if you do have time, try comparing some of their definitions with those found in the glossary in the back of a standard class text book. Quite often, pupils are pleased to discover that their own are fuller and easier to understand!

> The connections to improving literacy are clearly demonstrated here.

Resource 1

PRECIPITATION	EVAPORATION	INTERCEPTION STORAGE
rain	water	water
hail	kettle	leaves
snow	heat	branches
water	gas	trees
clouds	vapour	store
gas	steam	plants
condensation	bath	ground rain
liquid	shower	

TRANSPIRATION	DEPRESSION STORAGE	CONDENSATION
water	water	water
plants	surface	liquid
leaves	saturated	gas
sweat	soak	bath
breathe	lie	kettle
trees	puddle	steam
roots	ground	transfer
heat	pool	cold

EVAPO-TRANSPIRATION	GROUNDWATER FLOW	THROUGHFLOW
evaporation	transfer	soil
transpiration	water table	soak
water	rock	water
plants	aquifer	particles
leaves	move	transfer
sweat	flow	move
breathe	derain	infiltration
transfer	infiltration	earth

SURFACE RUN-OFF	INFILTRATION
water	water
ground	percolate
running	trickle
flowing	filter
over	spaces
top	into
move	soil
	ground

Settlement

Context

This is a development of *Exemplar 1* in which groups discuss and decide which words should be put on the card and made *taboo*. This version was designed for and trialled with a Y10 GCSE group that contained a fair sprinkling of less able pupils before using it with other classes. A large part of the term had been spent on a unit with a focus on settlement growth and change. With the end of year internal examinations approaching we used **Taboo** not only to refresh and reinforce topic related concepts but also to clarify the meanings and requirements of some of the command words used in exam questions. Candidates do not always appreciate what is required of them and examiners' reports at both GCSE and A Level often raise this as an issue.

Pupils were allowed to use their exercise books in the initial stage of this version of the game as it was unreasonable to expect them to remember in detail what the target words meant and so **Taboo** became an integral part of the revision process. If classes have already done some prior revision you can decide to do without the supporting resources.

One of my other classes had a somewhat erratic attendance record so I allowed them to use a standard textbook for additional support. Otherwise their ability to identify the target words from the descriptions provided by others would have been seriously limited!

> **Taboo** is an effective form of revision of the key words in topics.

Preparation

Nine target words per page, **Taboo** *Resource 2*, were printed onto paper then cut up into individual pieces. Each piece was blank apart from the target word. We made enough for two **Taboo** 'cards' per group but you can vary this in relation to the time you have available.

One problem that we had not anticipated was that some of the pupils' work required for these sessions was in full exercise books that they kept at home, so some of the pupils had to share with each other. Next time I remembered to forewarn them to bring them to school for the next lesson.

Provide a sheet of file paper for each group to write its ideas down.

Launching

I introduced the lesson as revision and examination preparation exercise. Pupils were told that the activity would help them to identify what they needed to revise on this subject and to check on some command words that come up in the exam. The winning group would be the one with the most points scored (as in *Exemplar 1*).

> Pupils do not generally associate revision exercises with enjoyment!

Instructions

1. Divide the class into groups of 3 or 4 pupils and give each one an identifying letter, A,B,C etc.
2. Give a slip to each group (or two each if you wish).
3. Give them 5 to 10 minutes to discuss the meaning of each key word and to list *all* the words they can think of that would help describe it.
4. Tell them that they now have to choose between 4 and 8 words from their list to be made **Taboo**.
5. Tell them that they should aim to make the most obvious ways to explain the key word difficult without making it impossible!
6. Groups should then write their chosen **Taboo** words on the slips of paper. At this point, tell them to put all books away.
7. Pass these on to the group with the next letter in the alphabet to their own with the last letter passing to group A.
8. Proceed as advised in *Exemplar 1* with each group having the task of producing an explanation for the key word without using the **Taboo** words generated by the previous group.
9. When you come to scoring, tell them that groups do not get a point for identifying their own key words! (There is always the possibility that they don't recognise another group's description, I suppose!)

Managing the activity

The tricky part of this version is in tempering the enthusiasm that some groups have for making their key word impossibly difficult to describe. You can always dream up a penalty system if a group is unable to construct a description at all without using *taboo* words, but I haven't had to do this yet. This reflects pupils' inventiveness! While circulating, it is a good idea to take a look at the *taboo* words being put on the slips. You can always take some 'editor's action' if need be or check that groups do have an understanding of a term. You can usually see from the shortness and content of their lists if they do not.

However from time to time a group will simply not understand the key word and cannot be bothered to find out. All is not lost. If the next group receives an inappropriate list of *taboo* words, accurate description is a piece of cake and the first group at least gets to hear what it really means!

Debriefing

Because pupils are selecting the words to made *taboo* they are choosing words that they think of using which may not be the same as ours. Dialect and slang may appear. The term 'gentrification' on more than one occasion has been explained with reference to the demolition of outside toilets, using some quite colourful language. Debriefing can be an opportunity to discuss the appropriateness of different forms of language in alternative contexts.

In response to the question 'How did you decide which words to make *taboo?*' groups said they found it hard but interesting to think of the different ways to describe the key word. They also had tried to anticipate how the next group might think and so to attempt to 'block' them. This had added an interesting twist to the task.

We also discussed what makes one word easier to describe than another and it boiled down to how well they understood the meaning of the key word. There had been some interesting whispered discussions. One had been over exactly what urbanisation meant, that just 'cities' wouldn't do. Those with limited understanding had difficulty finding 8 words to put in their initial list, so choosing which to put on the slip wasn't a problem, but the guessing was easier for the next group when it arrived with only a few *taboo* words on. In retrospect, I should have given the weak group more support.

Case studies proved popular ways of trying to get at the key word, drawing both on those I had introduced via previous lessons, but also some quoted examples from their own neighbourhoods which I wasn't aware of. Gentrification, for example was described as 'like what's going on where those skips are outside'.

Follow-up

As with *Exemplar 1*, groups worked together to prepare the best descriptions, explanations or definitions as briefly as they could.

Their results and the *taboo* words given by the other group are printed on *Resource 3* so that you can see how well it worked. This gives you a ready-made set of cards if you want to use the approach used in *Exemplar 1*. All you have to do is cut the explanations off the bottom of each slip. You could use these, of course, for a matching exercise on another occasion.

This monitoring is another example of diagnostic assessment.

This is Creative Thinking (NCTS) being employed in a somewhat unorthodox manner!

Pupils are constructing understanding through using what they know. They are going beyond learning the definition by establishing connections.

MIGRATION	COMPARE	SITE

EVALUATE	URBANISATION	GENTRIFICATION

SITUATION	SETTLEMENT	EXPLAIN

Resource 3

MIGRATION	COMPARE	SITE
Travel	Difference	Location
Moving	Similarities	Place
Location	Contrast	Area
Pull factors	Alike	Land
Push factors	Same	Directions
Quality of life	Looking	Functions
A term used for people perhaps using transport to go to another country maybe for a job.	Anthony has brown hair and Steven's is ginger. What am I doing to their hair colour?	This has been selected for building or usage due to its particularly suitable characteristics for that purpose.

EVALUATE	URBANISATION	GENTRIFICATION
Compare	Cities	T.W.D.C.
Contrast	Migration	Restoration
Value	Population	Old houses
	Rural	Refurbishment
	Shanty towns	Re-design
	Growth	New houses
	Movement	Better
	Town	Improve
To check over and verify something. To summarise and conclude. See if it is suitable for the task	Increasing numbers of people living in built-up, developed areas.	The upgrading of property

SITUATION	SETTLEMENT	EXPLAIN
Site	Town	Describe
Placed	Place	Annotate
Map	Area	Information
Area	City	Details
Atlas	Dwelling	Reasons
Location	Development	
Surrounded		
Where you or something else is in a region: inland, mountainous, flat etc.	Where people live; people's habitat; a location built for people to live in.	To analyse and conclude a final answer thoroughly.

Adapting the strategy

This is such an easy strategy to implement that a third Exemplar is unnecessary. The best are 'home made'.

You can also introduce another step by adding to their answers the **Taboo** words that they think actually *are* on the card: a useful check that they have got appropriate vocabulary. You can also try putting in the same word twice with a different set of **Taboo** words for a bit of fun!

Chapter 7

Layered Decision Making

7 Layered Decision Making

Rationale

Decision making is an increasingly important part of the geography curriculum at all secondary levels. It is a skill that is specifically mentioned in NC Key Stage 3, many GCSE syllabuses and most A Level syllabuses. Decision making exercises are becoming important components of the summative assessment process either in examinations or as part of coursework. Decision making often encourages the decision makers (pupils) to move along a well sign posted path, digesting data along the way, culminating in a decision. The process can often be unchallenging and simplistic.

The idea behind **Layered Decision Making** is to introduce the students to a more realistic, complex, challenging, unpredictable and even stressful process and make sense of it. Students make a series of decisions based on information available to them *at a particular time*. Data may change or be updated (new information introduced by the teacher) as the activity progresses. This more closely mirrors decision making in the real world. Thus the activity may challenge students' perceptions of the decision making process, skills in which can be developed with debriefing. Pupils are helped to understand how agreements are reached by introducing them to approaches to resolving conflict. (see *Resource 6*) These are useful in any decision making situation where conflicts of interest are key features. Following a decision, pupils can evaluate the pros and cons of the methods of conflict resolution they (or others) used and suggest alternatives.

This is a strategy that can vary enormously in scale and can be complicated for both teacher and pupils. If effectively debriefed, it can raise pupil awareness and understanding of the decision making process and lead to improved understanding of factors and variables which are important components of other Big Concepts: cause and effect, inequality, planning, development, and systems. Good debriefing can help them transfer their understanding of these ideas, both within and outside of the school curriculum. Potentially there are major benefits but they do have big implications for planning and implementation. We feel that the outcomes more than justify the effort of using the strategy.

Decision making is a high order thinking skill. It is one of geography's Big Concepts, and is specified in NC Geography KS3 2g. It features in several GCSE syllabuses and forms the basis of some of the synoptic papers at A Level. Ignore decision making at your pupils' peril!

It is an important dimension to becoming 'informed citizens' that pupils should develop a critical awareness of the processes at work that influence their lives at personal, neighbourhood and wider community scales.
(DfEE 1999 NC, pp 184,185)

Strategies such as 'Plus, Minus and Interesting' and 'Alternatives, Possibilities, Choices' can be introduced to help develop decision making skills (de Bono, 1992)

The closer simulations approach reality, the more complex they become.

Migration: The Stuarts Move House

Context

This activity involves students initially taking the role of David Stuart, the hero of the family, who has just landed a job in the North East (but it could be anywhere) and therefore needs to buy a house. There are two steps in the process. Pupils look at a range of (David's) criteria to make a decision. This then has to be reviewed when the students are made aware that the rest of the family is not entirely happy with David's decision because they have criteria of their own to be considered.

This activity has been used with a variety of ability levels in Y7, Y9 and Y10. It has been used both as part of a unit on settlement and a home region unit. The lesson this Exemplar describes involved a Y9 low-to-middle ability class studying a settlement unit. They were relatively well motivated but some needed support at times. The lesson was 60 minutes long.

This is one of the 'hooks' of this activity. It is rooted in the personal experiences of many pupils.

Preparation

Basic settlement 'theory' had already been studied and they had some understanding that the provision of services varies within cities and between urban and rural areas: ideas that featured in the discussions during this activity.

Preparation of resources was quite straightforward. Each group was given a copy of the instruction sheet (*Resource 1*), and to eliminate time wasted on 'busy' tasks, a comparison table (*Resource 4*) was made available. More able classes needed less help and were able to devise their own matrix. Each group also had a copy of *Resources 2 and 3*. It was also important to have copies of *Resource 5* ready for introduction at the appropriate time. It is easy to change the regional context by replacing the regional map then cut some house advertisements from your local free newspaper, and 'Bob's your uncle'. *Resources 1 and 5* make no reference to any particular region or city specifically so that you can use those directly.

Launching

Out of the blue I asked how they went about buying a pair of jeans. Roughly prioritised, they considered the label (how sad/cool), style, shop, fit and price. Clearly, teachers are in the wrong business. (I bet most readers at some time in their lives have worn something awful to be 'cool'. Go on. Admit it!) We recognised these things to be *criteria*. I then asked if any of them had ever moved house and why? The students' experiences were discussed in class and we explored the differences between moving around the corner and moving to a different part of the country and what were the most powerful factors (jobs and price).

There is more to this than surprise alone. It tries to connect the processes within pupils' experience to less familiar contexts.

The 'Moving House' sheet (*Resource 1*) was given out and the students asked to read through it. The key to a successful outcome for this activity is for decision making to be as realistic as possible. They need to identify with the principal character, so students were asked to think of themselves as David. It can be worthwhile getting them to close their eyes and imagine him and what he might think: what he looks like, what he does for a living, what music he likes etc.

This ability to empathise resonates with the objectives of the Personal, Social and Moral and Citizenship dimensions of the curriculum.

Instructions

The first part of the activity (David's decision) required little instruction. I gave out *Resources 1,2,3 and 4*. (I also used O.S. maps of the area (Landranger sheet 88.) *Resource 4* is a table and I told them that David's criteria for choosing a house were down the left hand side and the choice of houses along the top. If a house met one of the criteria then they were instructed to put a tick in the appropriate box. The house with the most ticks at the end would probably be the best (although see *Managing the activity* below). This part of the activity was then debriefed.

When the groups had made their decisions based on David's criteria list, it was time to introduce the element of conflict: David's family. Put simply, they didn't agree with David's choice of location. They all had their own ideas about the best place for the family, based on the demands of their own lifestyles. The key word now was 'compromise'. Students read 'The Hero Returns' (*Resource 5*) and the whole class considered this together. They were told that they had to form groups of 3 or 4 and each take the role of a family member and then to make another decision that would be acceptable to the whole family. I told them they could modify or even devise another matrix if they wished. Advice was given to groups as required.

Understanding negotiation processes helps pupils understand the real world outcomes.

Managing the activity

The activity was very carefully structured. The introduction set the scene for the lesson and introduced some of the key concepts being dealt with, and then the first part of the activity was done (relatively quickly) and debriefed. The first part was relatively straightforward. I monitored what was being done by who and how so that it could be used in the debriefing. I also helped any groups that were having difficulty. For example one group said that they thought that some of the criteria were more important than others. The 'problem' was resolved after discussion by making some of the criteria worth two ticks and others one tick. (I didn't use the term 'weighting', but perhaps should have done.)

The second part of the activity required little managing other than helping those that were struggling and keeping them on task. One of the key areas that pupils found difficult was carrying all the information in their head. Much of the help given was to prod them in the direction of ways to record preferences or modify the matrix. Most pupils would not know where, for example, all the swimming pools are within the region, so I made some old copies of Yellow Pages and Thompson's Local directory available. If you can get on the Internet pupils can search *Yell*.

Timings for the activity can vary depending on the ability level of the class and how many houses you choose to use. To fit this lesson into an hour I had to curtail both parts of the activity before most groups had considered all of the houses. Despite this I was still short of the amount of debriefing time I wanted! Vary the number of choices in relation to lesson length.

Follow-up

The most obvious way to follow this lesson up is to write up the decision and justify it. On this occasion I asked them to watch the TV News one night over the following week for a conflict and to write about one and to write about the approach(es) to conflict resolution that are being tried, or might be tried. (*Resource 6*)

Debriefing

The debriefing is an ongoing process in this activity. There are three main debriefing episodes.

At the start we looked at the students' experiences of moving house and at the important idea of criteria.

The second phase of the debriefing follows the first activity: that is David's decision on which house to buy. The main question to the pupils here is: '*How did you come to your decision?*'. We then discussed how their own family's criteria for house selection might vary. Once the 'The Hero Returns' sheet had been given out we discussed the idea that not all the family members would be happy with the decision as with most families, probably. I then asked (to liven proceedings up a little) what they thought the criteria that the Royle and the Royal family might be and how they would vary. This was where a pupil introduced the word 'compromise' (not an option in the Royle family). Just before doing the last part of the activity I gave them advanced warning that I would be asking how they came to a decision at the end of the lesson.

The third phase of the debriefing was based entirely on their ways of coming to the decision. It took quite a lot of time to go through this, a sign that the class were comfortable discussing these questions and ideas, but this left little time to summarise. With more time I would have used the 'Ways to Resolve Conflict' (*Resource 6*) and asked groups to identify the method of conflict resolution that they had used. This helps to build a decision making vocabulary. This slightly unpredictable dimension in which you cannot be sure what debriefing will throw up is part of both the learning and the enjoyment of *TTG*.

An appreciation of criteria is important for the development of Evaluation Skills (NCTS).

This is a common problem. Thumb-twiddling to fill the last five minutes tends not to occur. *TTG* activities are inherently differentiated and open and are capable of generating lively debate. Sometimes you have to pull hard on the reins to get debriefing in.

This is a conscious strategy to transfer understanding of the processes of conflict resolution to new contexts.

Another instance of the teacher expanding the pupils' awareness of the universality of decision making processes.

The Stuarts Move House

David Stuart (42) is a hero to his family: he has just landed an exciting new job as a nursing manager in a big regional hospital. He and his wife, Mary (37) have two lively children: Rachel (14) and Mark (12).

David has gone to sort out the details of his new job and to start looking for a suitable house. He has bought himself a map (Resource 2) and consulted the property section of the local newspaper (Resource 3). As he considers the available choices, he has the following criteria in mind:

● Within 50km of the hospital which is close to C.B.D.

● It must have 4 bedrooms

● It must be detached

● In a quiet area with a good sized garden

● Preferably in a pleasant village

● He likes the idea of an old house

● Within the price range £130,000 - £150,000

● Must have double garage

● Preferably within easy reach of the National Park as he is a keen hill walker in his spare time.

Study the details of the houses shown on David's shortlist (Resource 3) and his requirements above. Use the House Choice Matrix (Resource 4) to record with a **tick** a house that meets his requirements and an **X** if it definitely does not. You can put a **?** if it is not clear if a house meets a criterion or not.

Ask if there are any features of the houses that you are not familiar with.

Finally, total the ticks for each house.

Which is likely to be David's best choice?

Resource 2   ## Houses For Sale

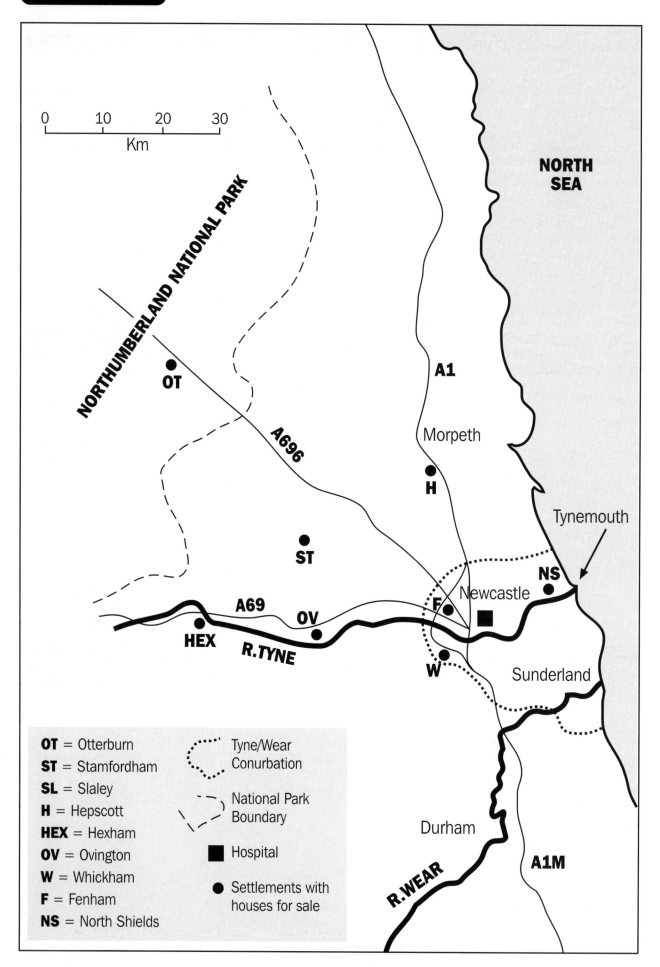

OT = Otterburn
ST = Stamfordham
SL = Slaley
H = Hepscott
HEX = Hexham
OV = Ovington
W = Whickham
F = Fenham
NS = North Shields

····· Tyne/Wear
      Conurbation

--- National Park
    Boundary

■ Hospital

● Settlements with
  houses for sale

Resource 3

STAMFORDHAM   1
Moor Farm

A productive smallholding with traditional period farmhouse and buildings offering an opportunity for equestrian or small scale agricultural use. Farmhouse: 4 bedrooms; 2 receptions; kitchen; bathroom; utility. Stone barn with granary; dairy; hay barn; calf house; garages.19 acres.

Offers in the region of
£150,000

OVINGTON   2

Unique period stone property retaining character of its era. Superb views over Tyne Valley. Accommodation comprising: lounge with stone inglenook fireplace, farmhouse kitchen/diner, utility, 4 bedrooms, 2 bathrooms, UPVC double glazed windows. Private garden.

£139,950

SLALEY   3

Detached family home situated in rural village south of Hexham with south facing views offering spacious accommodation: living room; dining room; study; kitchen; utility room; bathroom. Double garage. Gardens. Oil central heating.

£139,950

WHICKHAM   4
Fellside

Detached Dutch style bungalow. Gas C.H., some double glazing installed. Hall; lounge; dining room; conservatory; oak style fitted breakfasting kitchen; 2nd reception room; 3 bedrooms; bathroom; gardens; garage. Inc. carpets & curtains.

£160,000

HEXHAM   5
Beaumont Park

Delightful modern detached house occupying an elevated corner situation, offering family sized accom: entrance hall, cloaks/WC, 2 receptions, utility, breakfasting kitchen, 4 bedrooms, bathroom. Generous gardens, double garage. Gas C.H.

£129,500

HEPSCOTT   6
Nr. Morpeth

Delightful period residence, many features. 3 reception rooms, kitchen, breakfast room, master bedroom suite, three further bedrooms, bathroom. Double garage. Landscaped gardens. Part exchange will be considered.

Offers around
£170,000

NORTH SHIELDS   7
Dolphin Quay

Superb 4 bedroomed penthouse apartment on 4th floor with panoramic views over the River Tyne. Communal entrance door with 24 hour security camera, entryphone system & lift to 4th floor. Hallway leading to reception hall, delightful 22' lounge/dining room with river views & door to balcony, fully fitted Kitchen, furnished master bedroom with en suite bathroom and door to balcony, 3 further bedrooms (2 with range of fitted furniture and sharing an en suite bathroom), 3rd bathroom with peach coloured suite. Electric heating. Sealed unit double glazing. Garage and additional parking bay.

£145,000

FENHAM   8
Moorside South

Semi detached house with lovely gardens. Drive to double length garage with washroom and shower room/wc off. Entrance porch, reception hall, dining room, sitting room, breakfast room, kitchen. Four bedrooms, bathroom, wc, store cupboard. Gas heating. Burglar alarm.

£145,000

OTTERBURN   9
Detached Bungalow with Land

A most attractive modern stone built bungalow with 5 acres grazing land in a superb rural setting and commanding splendid views. Further adjoining grazing land can also be acquired. This property offering spacious accommodation may be of particular interest to those with horses.

OIR: £125,000

Resource 4

House Choice Matrix

David's criteria	1 Stamfordham Moor Farm	2 Ovington	3 Slaley	4 Whickham Fellside	5 Hexham Beaumont Park	6 Hepscott	7 North Shields Dolphin Quay	8 Fenham Moorside South	9 Otterburn
Within 50kms of the hospital in Newcastle?									
4 bedrooms?									
Detached?									
Price £130K-£150K?									
Double garage?									
Good sized garden?									
An old house?									
Easy reach of National Park?									
Total Ticks									

The Hero Returns!

David Stuart has returned to his family home in Leicester full of enthusiasm for the new home he has chosen. However, he has a shock in store: each member of his family disagrees with his choice.

In groups of 3 or 4, decide who will look at his choice from the point of view of each of the family members. They are:

> **MARY.** Mary is a solicitor's clerk. She can get a job in almost any town. However she had a car accident recently. Although she has recovered from her injuries, she has lost confidence in her driving. She wants a house within walking distance of work, school and shops. She would like a modern house that is easy to maintain and clean. She also insists on gas central heating and cooking.
>
> **RACHEL** (14). Rachel is unhappy about moving. She would really like to live in the country. She loves horse riding and wants a house with land, so that she can keep a horse. However she is beginning to be interested in going out in the evenings. She wants to leave home as soon as possible.
>
> **MARK** (12). Mark, a Leicester City supporter from birth, is a very good swimmer and has won many trophies. It is really important for him to live near a full sized swimming pool as he trains 3 times a week. He would like to live within easy reach of a Premiership football ground.

Resource 6   Ways to Resolve Conflict

In studying geography we often need to understand how things became the way they are and how they are going to change. If this involves people, it is pretty certain that there will be disagreement (conflict) between those with differing involvement in the issues (interest groups).

How conflicts are settled (resolved) depends on the strategy taken by the interest groups. At one extreme where there are big differences in power and influence between them, an interest group gets everything it wants at the expense of the others. At the other extreme, everyone gives and takes. In the end, the relative power of the interest groups, sometimes in the form of media influence, shapes the outcome. Often, conflicts are resolved using a combination of approaches.

Brute force	The person or interest group with the most power (sometimes physical) wins and takes all.
Amelioration	Winners take responsibility for softening the effects of change, eg, screening an ugly new building with an embankment and trees.
Compensation	Opposing interests are bought off by monetary or other tangible benefits.
Replacement	If change involves the loss of a particular asset such as a playground or wood, it may be reconstructed at a new location.
Timing	Different interest groups have access to the amenity (buildings or land) at different times.
Zoning	Interest groups agree to use different parts of the amenity.
Promises	One interest group may get its way by making promises of future actions of benefits to others, which may or may not be kept.
Legality	Laws may require or prevent change, irrespective of the wishes of the interest groups. (eg, demolition of an unsafe building or trade barriers and quotas)
Status quo	Nothing happens. The ideas for change are withdrawn.

Dam the Consequences

Context

The impact of change on economy, society and environment is a recurrent theme in geography and there are several published examples of decision making exercises, designed for different age groups concerning dams. This group activity has been used both with Y9 and A Level classes where the Amazonian rainforest ecosystem and the impacts of development on its indigenous people are studied. Older students bring more complex reasoning and draw upon more experience to reach more sophisticated decisions than younger pupils who do have a habit of taking somewhat extremist stances! In addition to highlighting the power of the profit motive and political interests, students confront their own values and attitudes towards civil rights, minorities, concepts of development and environmental conservation.

This particular version was used in a 40 minute lesson with a Y12 class of 14 students ranging in enthusiasm and ability from those intending to read geography at university to those taking the A Level to 'make up their timetable'. It is a complex process with three decision making layers but it can be run with surprisingly little background subject knowledge although the less they have, the more resources may need to be available to support their investigations as the activity does trigger a lot of questions! The focus is on the decision making process rather than content delivery. Debriefing can take longer than the activity itself.

This Exemplar is available in computer format at **www.chriskingtonpublishing.co.uk**. You may find it useful to try it out and familiarise yourself with it before using the paper based version. Alternatively, students can do the exercise for themselves in school or at home.

Preparation

This is crucial. Without it you can get yourself into an awful mess! However, the students need very little preparation. They have plenty of background knowledge of Amazonia. You do need to be clear which *Resources* to use when. One copy per group of each *Resource* needs to be printed even though some of the Level 2 and 3 Route sheets may not be used. It is very helpful if you can cut up and print each 'Level and Route' *Resource* on different coloured paper even though, to save space, we have put several on one page in this book. Familiarise yourself with the overall structure of the exercise:

Briefing (*Resource 7*)

Level 1 Decisions (*Resource 8*)

Choices:	• 'dispose' of problem villages	= Route 1
	• negotiate and rehouse villagers	= Route 2
	• stall the Government	= Route 3

Level 2 Decisions (*Resource 11*)

Options for Route 1	• no mercy, no survivors
	• gifts of infected clothing
	• destroy buildings only and hope they get the message
Options for Route 2	• bribe tribal elders to move
	• pay compensation and 'give' new sites
	• bring in government officials to move them for you.
Options for Route 3	• lie to government about geological unsuitability of site
	• be truthful and recommend building elsewhere

Level 3 Outcomes (*Resource 12*)

No choice for Route 1	• a leak to the press exposes your dastardly deeds
Options for Route 2	• elders refuse to move and want to tell the world of your plot.
	• relocation stories relating to alternative sites, A,B,C or D
	• Government says it is 'your problem'.

The accessibility of *TTG* strategies across the ability and age range is an advantage. They can be revisited (sometimes even the self-same one) and progression in pupils' reasoning becomes apparent.

This associates the notion of sustainable development with sustainable communities. There is a strong citizenship dimension to discussion in this Exemplar.

TTG encourages risk-taking for both pupils and teachers and not only in the cognitive sense!

Options for Route 3

- Government accepts excuse but will send team to investigate
- Government says that unless **you** do something they will cancel other project contracts they have with your company and you can kiss your profits goodbye.

Launching

I explained that all decisions have consequences, some intentional, some unexpected; some have positive outcomes, others, negative. Each outcome may be viewed as desirable by one interest group but negatively by another. I reminded them that Brazilian government policy has been to develop economic activity in Amazonia for many years including road building, forest clearance to create land for peasant farmers from other parts of Brazil, ranching, timber processing and mineral extraction. However, new developments need energy and if the forest itself is not to be exploited as a fuel source, some other means of energy production will be necessary. Any suggestions? We briefly discussed alternatives: Solar power: powerful sunshine but can be cloudy and only available for 12 hours a day; Wind? : likely to be irregular and squally; HEP? plentiful all year round. A good bet.

But good for whom? How might the indigenous population view such a development in their territory? I told the class that the objective of the lesson was to experience the decision making process in which they would represent the (fictitious) Brazil Power Corporation (BPC) which has been commissioned by the national Government in Brasilia to construct an HEP dam near Vera Cruz on the Purus river (a tributary of the Amazon) in the remote south west of Amazonas state. The recommended site for the dam is where the valley narrows sharply downstream of a broad gentle sided valley. The student's job is to decide how to implement the scheme against local opposition.

After refreshing memories about the variety of ways in which conflicts can be resolved (*Resource 6*) we were ready to roll.

Instructions

- Get the class into groups of 3 or 4, no more.
- Distribute *Resource 7* (briefing), and *Resource 9* (sketch map) to read carefully in groups.
- Discuss first reactions to the scheme.
- Give out *Resource 8* (Level 1 Decision sheet) to read and discuss. Introduce the Decision Mapping Matrix (*Resource 10*) and tell them to keep a detailed log of their decisions and reasoning in the *Before debriefing* columns of the sheet; and their evaluation of that decision after finding out what the consequences were throughout the activity in the remaining three columns: *After debriefing*.
- Give them about 5 minutes to reach their Level 1 decision and record it.
- Debrief this phase by asking whose interests they were really thinking about and what the consequences might be of the 3 different options.

The teacher's role gets a little interesting now!

- Tell them that now they have made one decision, they must deal with the consequences and that the way they deal with the next set of options at Level 2 will also have consequences at Level 3 too. Invite a representative from each group to collect from you the next piece of information. Select the Level 2 item that matches the Route number each group chose. (eg, if at Level 1, Route 2 was chosen, give out the Level 2 Route 2 item.
- The same representative should report the group's Level 2 decision to you in order to be given the appropriate Level 3 outcome. (eg, a group on Level 2 Route 2 that chooses option 3 would be given Level 3 Route 2 (see *Resource 12*) Outcome 3)
- Decide whether the class (or you) can cope with the option to review their decisions and backtrack a Level to change their previous decision.

Cause and effect is one of the Big Concepts and a major theme in *TTG* strategies.

The moral and ethical dimension to geographical issues is often avoided in the classroom, but geography is not value free: it can make a major contribution to the exploration of values and attitudes which is so important in students' personal development. There are strong links to the NC Citizenship curriculum here, too.

It should be noted that this is an imaginary scheme.

Managing the activity

The biggest risk to this activity is getting into a mess with the various pieces of paper, hence the advice about coloured paper or at least some prominent symbol in the corner of the *Resource*. Once underway, and each group is following its own Route, it isn't easy to stop it, so the introductory instructions must be clear. The teacher can be bombarded with demands for new data, so it is all but impossible to circulate to monitor the group discussions unless you base yourself at a desk or table in the middle of the working area and switch on your antennae. I would also advise running the activity with a small group before trying it with a large one!

Depending upon how thoroughly the groups discuss the options and their consequences before reaching a decision, this main phase can take anything between 10 and 20 minutes. Those coming up to you for the next Level data first may be asked to explain their reasoning to you. If you are not satisfied that they have thought about it seriously enough you can always ask a group to reconsider, not to change their decision necessarily, but to improve their arguments. You will have evidence of this from the notes they have made on the recording sheets. Sending one group back a step does seem to send a message to the others to be sure of their reasoning. It is not a competitive race to finish first.

You may also be asked lots of questions about the environment, or the practicalities of certain courses of action. Try to encourage them to talk through their thinking, rather than jump in to resolve the issue for them.

> Shallow thinking renders the activity pointless. Not all classes take to this kind of activity and some groups may need more motivating than others. It takes courage to abandon it, but if decisions are not being based on evaluation of the evidence, throw the towel in and put it down to experience!

Debriefing

Each student brings with them one or more personal mental models of the decision making process. Buying jeans or deciding which channel to watch on the family TV may use different approaches to those involving scenarios outside their personal experience in which the perspectives of interest groups may be more difficult to envisage. Younger students can relate more easily to the situation in *Exemplar 1* than in *Exemplar 2*. But in all cases, decision making requires the participant to de-centre and remove personal bias from the equation while appreciating the integrity of the motivation of other interest groups – however distasteful some of them may be. Some students bring with them some sophisticated models that they have developed through involvement in social activities both inside and outside school such as in drama clubs, youth clubs, Woodcraft Folk, team captaincy and cadets, as well as how issues are agreed within the family unit. These can be worthy of discussion in their own right.

> A strong Citizenship theme pervades this activity.

Debriefing this Exemplar, I first asked them to discuss in their groups a ranking of the interest groups in order of (perceived) power. I then asked them to consider where each interest group got its power from. This led to an interesting discussion of the legitimacy of Government in relation to the democratic system. Some students could not get beyond the notion that all politicians are 'in it for themselves' even though they could identify no personal gains other than re-election. Others could see that it is the role of Government to serve the national interest however that can be diversely defined. Many students had a gut reaction against the pursuit of profit by the power company without appreciating i) the company's responsibility to shareholders (whoever they might be) and ii) the role of profit in stimulating enterprise and wealth creation. One group suggested that the indigenous people might welcome 'development'.

> Here students are challenging implicit assumptions promoted by a variety of agencies including ourselves.

We explored the reasons why some of the groups had gone back a stage to change their decisions and they agreed that it was because they had not forecast what the outcome of their decision might be. As the activity had progressed some groups became more morally idealistic and defensive of minority interests, others more self-preservationist as they came 'under pressure' from the Government. The debrief wound up by recognising three things: that the more you know about the various sides of an issue, the better the decision you might make; that inequalities of power can lead to decisions that can severely disadvantage the weakest group; that in reality, you can't go back and change your decisions. You and others live with the consequences which throw up more decision making scenarios.

Some students got quite hot under the collar about some of the issues involved in this activity, especially when someone pointed out that HEP was a source of renewable energy

There is an abundance of ambiguity with data on this topic. At the time of writing there are still respected academics prepared to debunk global warming on national radio.

that produces no greenhouse gases and with rising sea levels, we (in Britain) should be welcoming it, not arguing against it. I was delighted that the activity had engaged their emotions as well as their reasoning and that they were transferring arguments between scales and contexts.

Follow-up

Students can reflect upon and evaluate the options provided at each Level. How realistic were they? What other possible choices might be available?

Afterthoughts

These Exemplars are, of course, imaginary. However, like more formal geographical models, they attempt to describe a generalised process. As such they provide a framework for examining case studies that draws attention to cause and effect, inequalities of power in the decision making process, and the complexity of factors at work, albeit rather polarised to make them more 'visible'.

Briefing

We Understand Power

Group briefing

You represent the Brazil Power Corporation, a highly profitable company that specialises in HEP production and the construction of massive dams and reservoirs. You have a reputation for 'getting results' in difficult circumstances.

Government fieldwork has established a suitable site and has contracted you to build a large HEP station at Vera Cruz, in a remote and undeveloped region of Amazonas state. It is hoped that this will stimulate economic development in the region. As a major plank of Government regional development policy, it must be a success. You are under pressure to make the right decisions but you have some freedom to adapt the scale of the project to suit local circumstances. However, potential profits are in relation to the size of the scheme.

Resource 8

Level 1 Decision

Your company has accepted the contract to construct the Vera Cruz HEP dam and reservoir but the Government only gave you a simple map of the area that may be flooded and little else, so you sent your own team of consultants to find out more. Here is their report.

Consultants' report:

The valley that is proposed to be flooded is home to a number of tribes of indigenous people, only one of whom speaks Portuguese. They have lived for generations in the rainforest, untouched by the outside world, though one or two have acquired T-shirts and a framed picture of Sting from somewhere. They are completely dependent on the forest for their livelihood and survival. At present they have no concept of or use for electricity.

The population of the valley is roughly 6000, and at the moment it is difficult to say how they will react to our plans to dam the river and flood their land, but they don't look too threatening. We recommend that for economies of scale the project should be as big as possible.

Study the map to see where the consultants have found tribal settlements. Consider whether or not they all need be affected.

You may now proceed with the first decision. You have these three choices. Under no circumstances should the general public get to hear about any of this.

STRICTLY CONFIDENTIAL
Route 1 A group of rough looking characters has approached your consultants as they were leaving the site in their jeep. They have offered a quick solution. For a price, they get rid of the villages for you and cover up all trace of your involvement. Do you trust them?
Route 2 You can try to persuade the villagers to move to a new location out of the way of the reservoir. However, this could attract the interest and objection of environmental pressure groups if they found out how much forest would be lost and how many people displaced.
Route 3 You could delay starting the project, stall the Government with 'engineering problems' and wait for a less complicated project to come along.

The Dam at Vera Cruz

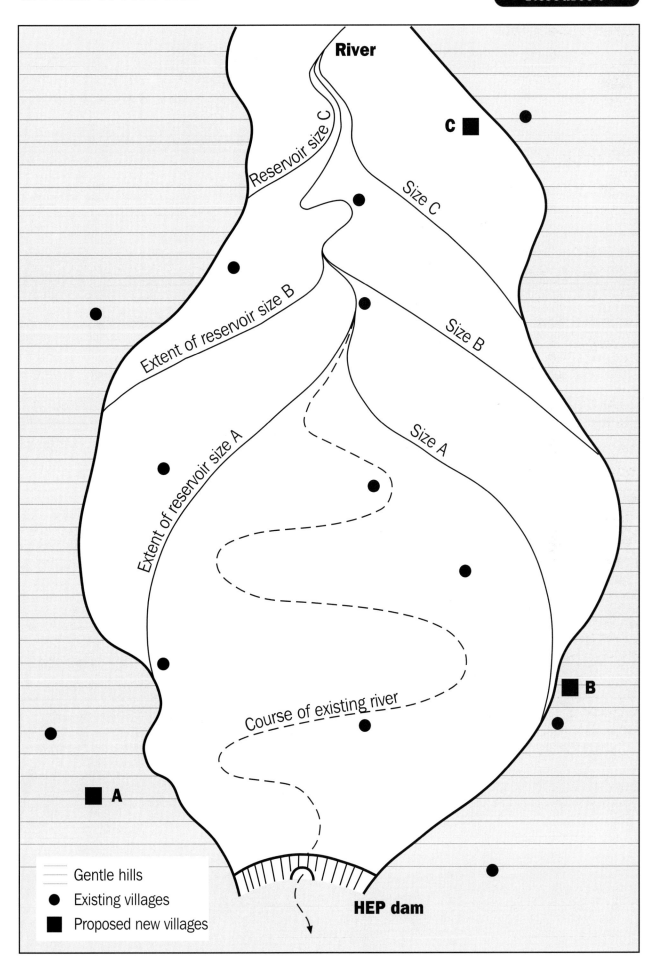

River

Reservoir size C

C ■

Size C

Extent of reservoir size B

Size B

Extent of reservoir size A

Size A

Course of existing river

■ B

■ A

Gentle hills

● Existing villages

■ Proposed new villages

HEP dam

Resource 10

Decision Mapping Matrix

Decision No		BEFORE DEBRIEFING		AFTER DEBRIEFING		
		Choice	Why take that decision?	What happened as a result of this decision?	Was it a good or bad choice? Why?	What other information would have been helpful?
1						
2						
3						
4						

Level 2 Decisions

Level 2 Route 1

You have opted to take the advice of your 'local contractors' and 'dispose' of the problem villages. You must choose one of 3 ways of doing this. Alternatively, you could go back and change your first decision.

Option 1

Employ the local thugs to wipe out the villagers and their inhabitants by burning houses, destroying their few crops and shooting the people, leaving no survivors to tell of your butchery. The problem simply goes away.

Option 2

To appear innocent of wrongdoing, contractors could offer gifts such as items of clothing which have been infected with diseases to which the tribes have no immunity.

Option 3

Employ contractors to destroy the village buildings only to leave the tribespeople homeless and too frightened to stay.

Level 2 Route 2

You have opted to try to move the tribes to locations outside the planned flooded area. You have 3 ways to achieve this:

Option 1

The tribal elders have requested a meeting to discuss the project and the effect on their valley. The other villagers will do as they say, so you can try to bribe them personally with gifts such as a Rolex copy and 'western' clothing. This is a low cost option. Will they fall for it and leave?

Option 2

You fear that the villagers will be reluctant and find it difficult to leave without your support. You get your contractors to prepare sites well above the lake level with their heavy equipment and offer to transport all the villagers' belongings for them. The contractors' skills would be used to help construct new buildings at the new sites.

Option 3

You inform the Government that you cannot proceed with the scheme until the villagers have been evicted and you request that personnel be sent to carry out the eviction. This is not the responsibility of a power company.

Level 2 Route 3

You have chosen to stall the Government and must find a way to buy time. You have 2 options:

Option 1

Progress hinges on the completion of an accurate geological survey of the valley. (Early results look good) You can tell the Government that the density of the forest, illness among the geologists and the need for spares for the Jeep have seriously slowed progress.

Option 2

Tell the Government the truth about the villages. You recommend that the dam should be built in another valley.

Resource 12   Level 3 Outcomes

Level 3 Route 1

You chose to 'dispose' of the problem tribespeople and their villages by one of the methods suggested by your contractors. Somehow, news of your actions has reached the press. A 'friendly' journalist in the newspaper office in Brasilia faxes you the following message:

> 'One of our reporters says she is on to a big story involving BPC: something about massacres and burning villages around Santa Cruz. She says all she needs is an eye witness account and she'd be ready to publish. She has asked the boss for permission to charter a Cessna to fly her up the Purus valley from Manaus.'

You can't think how that got out, but as sure as nuts come from Brazil, you know it will be international headline news. Your company is on the verge of a public relations disaster.

Level 3 Route 2

Option 1

You have chosen to try and bribe the elders to move their entire villages elsewhere. They are all outraged that you should suggest they abandon their spiritual homes and the resting place of generations of ancestors, only to drown them. They would rather fight and die than move. They will tell all the neighbouring villages and contact one of their sons who left to work in Manaus to tell the world about it.

Level 3 Route 2

Option 2

You chose to compensate and relocate the villages.

The following are transcriptions of national TV news reports by journalists visiting two villages a year or so after the move.

First village: 'Where we used to live is under water now that the Big Lake has filled the valley. Since moving here, life has been miserable. We have no river near us to fish in and we spend much time walking to fetch water. You have to use it carefully or wait for the afternoon rains to wash ourselves. They told us nobody else lived here, but other tribes hunted for animals and gathered food from this area and we had many arguments and even fights about that. There don't seem to be so many animals to hunt as there were. The soil is not as fertile either. It can't be so many years since other people cleared and cultivated the land because the forest round here isn't fully grown. The company just dumped us here and left.'

Second village: 'When the power company came to move us with their tractors and trailers, of course we were sad to leave, but we have moved our village before when the soil around us wasn't growing good crops any more. With their modern machines they cleared the forest in no time and cut timbers to build new homes for us. They had pushed a roadway from the lake to our site so it's not too difficult for us to get to the water to fish, wash and trade some of the products of the forest with boats coming along the river. We can even trade things we make with the workers' store at the dam site. The company even gave us some tools to make our work easier.'

Level 3 Outcomes, continued

Level 3 Route 2

Option 3

You have decided to let the Government handle the relocation of the villages.

It responds to your request in a most decisive manner. Part of its letter reads:

> 'We regret that you find it difficult to move these few villagers. You will not need reminding of the clause in your contract which refers to.. *removal of obstacles to the completion of the project.* If you cannot proceed as per contract then it will be terminated and advance payments to BPC will have to be reimbursed.'

The prosperity of the company is in jeopardy. You cannot afford to lose this contract.

Level 3 Route 3

Option 1

You have told the Government that your geological survey team has encountered a number of difficulties that has put progress seriously behind schedule.

The Government response is unexpectedly and uncharacteristically helpful.

Its e-mail message to your head office reads:

> 'We are disappointed at the lack of progress but fully understand the problems of working in such remote and difficult territory. As we wish to have the dam complete before the elections in 3 years time, we are dispatching a team from the Brazilian Geological Survey to support your efforts. They and their equipment should arrive by helicopter from Manaus on Thursday.'

Level 3 Route 3

Option 2

You have been truthful with the Government about the situation regarding the tribal villages and you have recommended that the HEP project be moved to another valley.

The Government response to your message arrives quickly by way of a 'phone call' from the Energy minister, Rosa Sanchez. She makes the Government's position clear:

> '...doesn't seem to have been a problem in the past does it? Or do you need reminding of the Earthwatch campaigners' photographs of your employees up to no good in Amapa state that the Public Prosecutor has on file? Unless BPC improves its powers of persuasion there really isn't much point in awarding it contracts, is there? We need results. The electorate expects them.'
> (click)

| Exemplar 3 | # A New Stadium for Middleton United? |

Context

This Exemplar is computer-based in Internet format. It can be accessed at **www.chriskingtonpublishing.co.uk.** It comprises **four** Levels of decision making that are ultimately judged by an 'Independent Adviser'. It has been trialled in Y9, Y11 and at A Level. It is structured like *Exemplar 2* but it avoids the practical problems of paper management! It reduces student movement around the room and frees the teacher to play a 'sweeper's' role. This is an account of using it with an A Level group. The topic emerged from the public controversy about Newcastle United's plans to build a new stadium on a public park adjacent to the present ground. This Middleton United Exemplar is modelled on the 'original'.

Preparation

If you are lucky to be on-line in your teaching room you can organise this activity for pairs of students to use the terminal in turn, then debrief when they have all had a go. Otherwise you will need to book your Internet linked computer suite for a lesson.

Other preparation is minimal if being used to introduce the complexity of decision making. Prior knowledge of the nature of conflict and approaches to resolving it is useful but not a pre-requisite. Indeed, it can be one of the main outcomes. An interest in the 'beautiful game' is an intended hook. A show of hands established that as many of the girls as boys were supporters of one club or another. Those without an interest in the game usually associate themselves with one of the other interest groups opposing the proposal, so they weren't marginalised.

> This should not be undertaken lightly. It requires much of the teacher in terms of considering ranges of possible (realistic) options open to the consequences of past decisions, much as **Mysteries** involve constructing a variety of ways in which an outcome could be reached.

Preparation of the resources proved to be a herculean task and required web-authoring skills, but I know the students have benefitted from using it and the trials and tribulations of setting it up will have been worth it if other teachers and students try and enjoy it. Students only require the ability to use *simple* Internet functions and a copy of *Resource 10*. You, on the other hand, are strongly advised to try the activity out for yourself first!

Launching

This topic needed little introduction because of its earlier regular exposure on regional TV. Launching it today, I would refer to recent legal battles between the club and season ticket holders who look set to be booted out of their regular seats to make way for corporate hospitality suites. 'Foul', cried the supporters. Perhaps this conflict could be avoided if the club was allowed to build a new stadium......! Any introductory discussion on a local planning issue will serve as well. Establishing what they do know about the planning / decision making process is very important.

I asked the students to look carefully at screens 1 and 2 (*Resource 13*) and then predict the outcome. I ask them to record it on paper together with their reasons, for use during debriefing.

Instructions

1 Get the class into pairs and tell them that ideally time spent with pencil and mouse should be equally shared.

2 After logging on and arriving at the start, it is wise to take them through the objectives and guide them through the first two screens so they are aware of their role.

3 Issue *Resource 10* which has 5 blank columns in which they record their choice at each level of decision making. They should fill in the first two columns first. After confirming their decision and discovering the (computer's) response to it, they should then discuss and fill in their reactions to it in the three right hand columns.

> This is hitting a variety of geography, citizenship, and NCTS targets.

4 Encourage them to explore the opinions of interest groups / individuals which reflect a range of support and objection to the plans (left hand column of screen).

5 Once decided and recorded (but **not before**) students can click on their choice to see the consequences. They must now **reflect** on their decision and complete remaining columns.

6 Now that they have the idea of how it works, they may proceed at their own pace, discussing and recording as they go until the 'Independent Adviser' makes a final decision.

Unlike the other two Exemplars, students cannot retrace their steps. Debriefing usually reveals the frustration that accompanies the evaluations of their decisions after the outcomes are known.

Managing the activity

Students remain seated throughout. They must be guided through the first decision layer to establish procedure. Thereafter you can support each pair as necessary. It is useful to pick up on some of their behaviours, especially frustration at not getting their own way and discussion of various approaches to conflict resolution.

Debriefing

The aim is for students to understand that in complex decision making it is likely that the interests of any one group will not be completely satisfied. Some concessions are inevitable. I used a number of questions to help analyse the process:

- What did you predict the outcome to be?
- Was that the outcome and if not why not?
- What is your response to the outcome? Was it fair and reasonable?
- How would you re-route your decisions if you could?
- How did you and your partner(s) reach agreements?
- What other methods might you have used to persuade your partner(s) to accept your point of view?

Most students disagreed with the Independent Adviser's final decision. One said,

> 'I felt we were prepared to compromise but environmental pressure groups weren't. I didn't expect them to refuse to compromise. They just rail-roaded their ideas through. The plan isn't ours any more.'

The exercise results in the rejection of the stadium proposals which frustrated the pro-development preferences of many males in the group. The plan does not proceed without consultation so they are forced to reconsider the views of others. Many reported that they were prepared to 'soften' the effects of the stadium on the neighbourhood (amelioration). As a final discussion point, I asked them to think of other situations in which they had had to make concessions or offer some form of compensation (or other forms of conflict resolution) in order to get their own way. There was no shortage of ideas here!

> As adults, negotiating skills are essential. Many of the skills are, of course, honed during adolescence in a domestic context!.

Follow-up

This was in the form of an extended written piece entitled 'Should Middleton United build a new stadium?' I invited them to include an appraisal of what the consequences of *not* building one might be (the 'do nothing' option). It could also form the basis of a cost/benefit analysis exercise.

There is scope to use this activity as a springboard to explore other conflicts or the work of pressure groups and the ways in which influence of less powerful interest groups can be enhanced eg, through media management.

Adapting the strategy

Any situation where change involves conflicts of interest can be shaped into a layered decision making activity, be it cinema or supermarket developments, third world debt or going organic. Each depends on the combination of a proposal, a number of more or less incompatible interest groups and an outcome.

Best of luck!

Resource 13

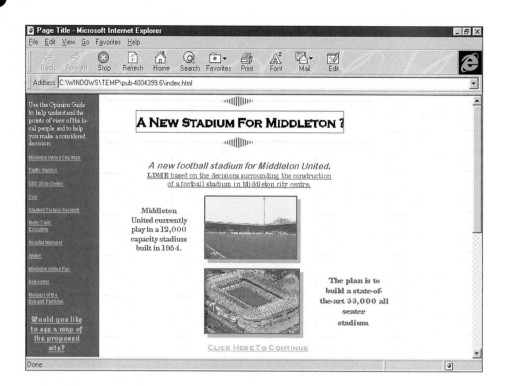

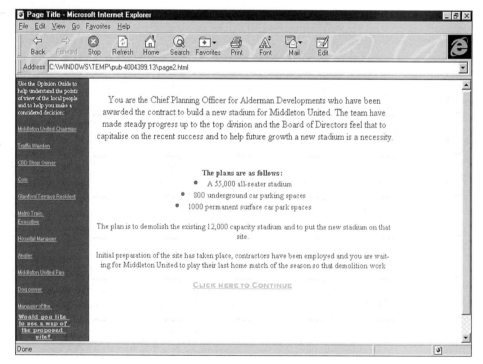

Chapter 8

Concept Maps

8 Concept Maps

Rationale

Concept Maps are an interesting way of helping pupils to make sense of complexity, marshal their ideas and ultimately produce more coherent and sophisticated explanations of geographical patterns, processes and events. Groups of pupils are given between 6 and 16 concept slips or cards which are spread about on a piece of A3 or sugar paper. Pupils are then required to make links between two concepts with a line and a definition or explanation of this link. The quality of the **Concept Map** is related to the quantity and quality of the links. Pupils explore the inter-relationships between the parts to gain a fuller understanding of and to be able to explain the whole.

Concept Maps have become regular features of teaching and learning in many geography departments following the publication of *Key Stage 3 Optional Tests and Tasks Unit 2: Earthquakes Task 2* (SCAA, 1996) where the strategy focused on the Kobe Earthquake **Mystery**. This was devised by the *Thinking Through Geography* Group.

Unlike brainstormed spider diagrams which aim to amass as much information as possible in an undifferentiated way, **Concept Maps** are graphic organisers of the relationships between the component concepts embedded in a theme or issue.

Concept Maps are one way of raising the profile of the process of explaining. They can be used at the start of a topic to tease out pupils' existing knowledge and understanding, or at later stages to synthesise and organise new or extended understanding. They have a number of other advantages:

- They focus on one of the most important of geography's Big Concepts: cause and effect.
- They are visual organisers and summarisers of information which most pupils find helpful in committing ideas to memory.
- They can be a valuable planning tool for pupils in organising extended writing (comparing and explaining skills, for example).
- They are an excellent approach to differentiation in that the activity is accessible to all pupils through discussion and pupils are free to organise their **Concept Maps** in any way that makes sense to them. The number and quality of links will vary; and no two **Concept Maps** will be the same.
- They are challenging. Pupils must identify which factors or concepts are related and establish how. This involves deductive and inductive reasoning and speculation.
- They are a powerful tool for diagnostic assessment. You can readily interpret the level of understanding of the topic through them.
- And lastly, if somewhat frivolously, they make eye-catching wall displays of pupils' work at any time of year, not just when 'an inspector calls'!

Many teachers use them in designing the units of work. How did we ever live without them?

NCTS Information Processing is a strong feature of this strategy. Such concrete 'manipulatives' can be highly effective if combined with discussion (Olsen & Gee,1991). For a deeper insight, see Ghaye & Robinson (1989)

The principles and practice of their use are explored by Leat & Chandler, in *Teaching Geography 21(3)* 1996

Establishing links is a crucial step in developing Reasoning Skills (NCTS) which move pupils forward from simply describing to the higher order cognitive process of explaining.

This appeals to the visual/spatial ways of learning that help to make abstract relationships more concrete.

More Thinking Through Geography

Comparing Earthquakes

Context

My below average ability Y9 class had already studied volcanoes and everyone had some prior knowledge of earthquakes. There had been one 'standard' lesson on their distribution and physical causes and a second comparing and contrasting the San Francisco earthquake of 1989 with the Turkish earthquake of August 17th 1999 which was still fresh in many pupils' minds. I used video clips of BBC News and Waugh and Bushel's *Interactions* pp 24-25 for San Francisco. The Turkish earthquake resource *(Resource 1)* is based upon a newspaper report. The pictures *(Resource 2)* are freely available on the Web (www.neic.usgs.gov/neis) and excellent supplementary material for class use can be found in Hopkin, 2000.

The next objective was to understand how humans interact with such hazards and why the effects vary in different parts of the world.

They had not done **Concept Maps** before, so I decided to provide support by structuring the early stages of the activity, then let them get on with it once they had a firm grasp of procedure. (This wasn't necessary later on in the year when we concept mapped again). The incentive to take the activity seriously was that the follow-up tasks would form part of their KS3 portfolio of assessed work.

Preparation

The first step was to identify the concepts or influential factors involved in the theme or issue. Some were specific to this particular earthquake, but it was important to include those factors that would play a part in the events surrounding *any* earthquake so that generalisations can be considered and made. In the planning stage, I jotted down all the information and ideas involved in the lesson in groups on paper and then gave the groups headings. For example, details of how crowded the streets were, whether people were at work, in schools, on holiday and so on we gathered under the factor heading of 'time of earthquake'.

These concepts were typed up, printed on A4 paper, cut up and a set put into an envelope for each group of pupils. *(Resource 3)* A blank piece was included so that pupils could incorporate ideas that they might have acquired from outside the classroom. Incidentally, I have used the terms *concepts* and *factors* interchangeably.

I organised pupils into groups of 3 or 4 in friendship groups. Each group was given an envelope of concept slips, a sheet of light-coloured sugar paper, a glue stick, ordinary pens to write with (they don't always bring their own!), text books, an atlas and copies of the *Resource* sheets. The newspaper report had been re-written to make the language more accessible for those with low levels of literacy.

Launching

We refreshed our memories about the world distribution of volcanoes and earthquakes and discussed whether or not all such events are disastrous. There was general agreement that they would be if people or property were destroyed or damaged. I explained that the aim of the lesson was to explore the issue in the form of an Enquiry question: *'Would a wealthy, developed country suffer more or less than a poorer, economically less developed country if hit by earthquakes of the same intensity?'* I gave the groups a couple of minutes to ponder. *'Think about the two examples of earthquakes we already know something about'.* The question soon provoked quite an argument which revealed some highly materialistic values held by some pupils while others with stronger social consciences felt it would be worse for the poor who would be left destitute and hopeless by losing what little they had. One hard-nosed boy who said that the poor would be used to going without was criticised for being mean.

News reports tend to dramatise death statistics as if they were more important than the people they represent. Some textbooks even list the dead in earthquakes like a macabre league table. Not all teachers feel comfortable stimulating emotional responses in the classroom, but then it is the human drama surrounding disasters that seems to excite pupils' interest. Pupils should appreciate that disasters are not arcade games or movies. Real people experience misery, pain and losses. Geography is classed as a Humanity, isn't it?

The immediacy with which teachers can respond to events enhances the impact and relevance of the topic to the pupils. Videos of day to day news broadcasts are obvious candidates for **Predicting with Video**.

Any earthquake could be considered in relation to the concepts on the *Resource* sheet. It is easy to incorporate this *TTG* activity into Unit 21 Virtual Volcanoes and Internet Earthquakes of the QCA KS3 schemes of work (QCA, 2000). **5W** could also be used here.

This is a fine example of scaffolding where teacher support is progressively removed as pupils are able to stand on their own feet.

This can be a particular problem with Internet sources but the capacity to download electronic text makes editing to differentiate the resource much easier than working with newspaper cuttings.

By challenging pupils to de-centre and by engaging them affectively through such activities, this strongly touches NC Citizenship 3a.

Instructions

1 I started by asking what they thought the two case studies had in common. *'Chaos. Dead and injured. Panic. Smashed buildings. People pulling away at rubble. Roads blocked'* came the replies. Then I asked what was different. *'Cars. Buses. Bikes. Clothing. Houses. Fire engines. The numbers of dead. The cost of the damage,'* to name but a few.

The teacher frames the task as a comparing and contrasting activity but it also involves the transfer of ideas from one context to another.

I then said: *'OK. We've found out a lot about the earthquakes in San Francisco and Turkey from the videos, text book and newspaper articles. Now I want you to think about why the effects of an earthquake might be worse in one part of the world compared to another. The concepts on the slips of paper in the envelope have all got something to do with it, but there may be some other factors that I haven't thought of because I was preparing this late last night when I was a bit tired. So if there is something else that you think is important, just let me know and I'll help you decide whether you should put it on the blank piece.'*

This seemed to set the tone of the activity (in common with a number of Thinking Skills strategies) that not everything pupils need is automatically provided and that there might not be enough evidence to be sure of a link.

2 After asking if they understood the meanings of the words on each slip of paper in the envelope, they were told to spread the concepts out around the sugar paper.

There is a tendency simply to state the link with words like 'affects', and 'causes'. The use of demonstrators makes explicit the teacher's level of expectation which will vary in relation to the ability range of the class.

3 I read out one of the demonstrator explanation links and asked pupils to spot which two concepts or factors were linked by that explanation, then to stick them to the sugar paper, linked by a line. The demonstrator explanation was then stuck along it. This process was repeated with the other explanations.

4 I then set them going to find and explain as many links as they could on their own and that notes would do, stressing that it was the quality of the explanations that mattered and that any factor may be linked to a number of others. I gave them 15 minutes for this.

5 To establish that there may be several links to any one factor, ask if anybody could see another link for, say, the magnitude of the earthquake. They came up with a variety of reasoned connections. With more able groups they may provide quite lengthy explanations and more links than you ever imagined possible, sometimes a bit wacky.

Managing the activity

This confirmed the openness of the task.

This is a really easy activity to manage, but you need to keep an eye out for the groups that are simply stating that there *is* a link. I usually ask them why or how does x link with y and then tell them to write *that* down.

In such circumstances they are articulating some of their attempts to extend their reasoning into unknown territory. As such it exemplifies NCTS Creative Thinking.

Some groups start by drawing lots of linking lines first (characterised by dialogue such as *'This and this, this and that, that and that'*) and write explanations later. However, watch out for those who first draw a complete web of *all* concepts interlinked. Sometimes they waste time struggling to find a reason for a link when one may not exist. Encourage them to start with the more obvious ones.

The teacher is attempting to introduce some organisation into what may be a random process for some pupils.

Having ignored one of my previous instructions, one group proceeded to connect the factors up in a linear sequence, using each factor only once. I picked two that they had not joined directly and asked how they might be linked, reminding them of a scene in the video where one building stood untouched beside the heap of rubble of another. They seemed happy *not* to be constrained by sequencing.

Pupils here are actually trying to do what TT promotes: transferring a strategy learned previously to a new situation. Left to their own devices they would ultimately have discovered it to be an inappropriate one here.

I overheard some interesting discussion which indicated that the rich world/poor world contrast was not being taken as cut and dried. One example was a group discussing the relative adequacy of emergency services. *'The rich countries have plenty of fire engines and ambulances and things like that'* said one girl, who was challenged by a boy in the group: *'Aye, but they are not much use if the roads are full of rubble and broken glass. (pause) ...but they'd have more JCBs to dig it away, though. Girl: Yeah, but what if the hospitals and fire station collapse like those buildings in the video? The doctors might get killed too.'* If you can hear 'ifs' and 'buts' it is usually a sign that they are openly testing hypotheses and realising that conclusions are not as predictable as they might have thought.

This is a significant step: pupils are evaluating evidence by exploring the ambiguity of the data.

I gave them a one minute warning to stop when I saw that two groups had milked all their sensible explanations dry and were starting to be over-inventive!

I could hear one group wondering aloud if it was safer in the country than the city. They argued convincingly that urban areas are congested with tall buildings whereas in rural areas there would be fewer concrete or brick buildings and glass to fall on you. I suggested that they use a blank slip for *Urban* or *Rural* and left them to it. If I had pressed them, they might have also drawn upon and used their knowledge that most wealthy countries have highly urbanised populations. Most groups could not find data about geology or relief but realised the hazards of living on a steep slope! One group came up with 'media coverage' as a factor in gathering resources to help in rescue efforts and put that on their blank slip.

Knowing what pupils need to find out is an element in Enquiry skills and is further explored in **5W**.

Debriefing

This was the group's first encounter with **Concept Maps**. I was really impressed by how well they took to it.

We discussed:

- *Which factors do you think are most important in influencing the impact of an earthquake?* Most thought it was to do with wealth.

- *How did you reach this conclusion?* They generally agreed that it was the factors with the most connecting links, though one group said it should be the ones they had written most about.

- *Why did you disagree sometimes?* Their responses to this question boiled down to a realisation that the same factor could sometimes work positively and negatively towards the outcome. For example, if the earthquake struck during rush hours people might not be inside the buildings that collapse. On the other hand they could be hit by falling debris, derailed in a train or in a car on a collapsed fly-over.

Further appreciation of the ambiguity of some data.

- *Did the disagreements help you understand anything?* Yes, that more than one view point can be right.

I would have liked to discuss the effectiveness of the given factors in enabling them to find 'homes' for all their ideas, but the end of the lessons was looming, so I jumped to my last question:

- *How could you make use of a **Concept Map?*** Other than '*put it on the wall*' this question was still-born because I'm not sure they had ever felt the need for one! However, the **follow-up** activity gave them an idea.

Debriefing attempts to make explicit the processes involved in the activity, but pupils do not always appreciate the contribution it can make to their learning.

The homework I set was a prelude to the assessment tasks. I asked them to write down their ideas about the following question: *In which of the two case studies would the country be able to recover from an earthquake disaster more quickly and why?* This was to start them thinking about short and long term effects and responses to the disaster.

Follow-up

In the following lesson, the class was introduced to the written assessment tasks. Taking one example of an earthquake to hit a wealthy country and one in a less economically developed country, these were followed by two reports about the situation in each case six months later. If you let the pupils choose the audience they are writing for (for example a national newspaper, an international emergency relief agency or the Government of the country) you have differentiation by outcome.

The main benefit of returning to the **Concept Map** at this point is to allow them to discuss *how* they are going to write their reports so that they are logical and coherent. Some of the best reports had chosen the concept that they had singled out to put in the middle of the web as a starting point to write about first and then bring in each of the others to which it was connected.

This is a form of drafting; a key element in the writing process.

As an alternative to report writing, pupils can draw their own **Concept Map** for one particular earthquake incorporating more case-specific information. I have also used the **Concept Map** with some success as a basis for speculating what would happen if an earthquake hit our own home region.

This is another attempt to encourage contextual transfer.

There are some wonderful opportunities for increasing differentiation still further by incorporating the use of **ICT** in this activity in two ways. Firstly, the World Wide Web has a wealth of good sites on tectonics that enable pupils to research their own case studies. Some are listed in the Resources section of QCA's Unit 21. However, the United States

Geological Survey National Earthquake Information Center is an outstanding site giving details of earthquakes past and present including maps and photographs. My pupils are fascinated by the daily list of events and locations which can be a useful point of reference for the discussion question 'When is an earthquake a disaster?' mentioned earlier. (www.neic.usgs.gov/neis)

Newspaper reports are easy to find **www.guardian.co.uk** is really easy to use. Select **search the archive** in the **go to** drop down menu, and search for 'Turkey earthquake'.

The second use of ICT can be in the construction of the **Concept Map** itself using text boxes, lines and arrow heads. Real sophisticates can even insert hot-links to websites!

Thousands killed and injured as earthquake shakes Turkey

A POWERFUL earthquake struck at least four cities in western Turkey early today. The death toll stood at 1,173 by 5pm today with over 5000 injured and is likely to rise steeply while rescue operations get underway. Thousands of homes collapsed under the force of the earthquake, which registered at least 6.7 on the Richter scale.

The earthquake hit at 3am, flattening buildings in towns and cities around the eastern end of the Marmara Sea. Many of the dead were crushed in their sleep. In the hard-hit town of Golcuk, the mayor said 500 buildings housing 2,000 families had collapsed with as many as 10,000 people under the debris," The dead included 160 members of the Armed Forces who perished in the collapse of two buildings in Golcuk,

some 81 miles (130 kilometres) southeast of Istanbul. Hundreds of people were also reported injured in the western cities of Bursa, Eskisehir, Bolu and Yalova. Thousands of people in towns and villages took to the streets in panic and spent the rest of the night outdoors.

"We need everything: field hospitals, kitchens, tents and ambulances," governor Nihat Ozgol said in Yalova, where 90 people died. A dozen hours after the quake, many victims remained buried in the rubble of their homes and rescuers have been digging with everything from bare hands to picks and shovels. "They can hear the voices of my mother and sister but know nothing about my father and brother," said Arsu Yilmaz as rescue workers dug at a

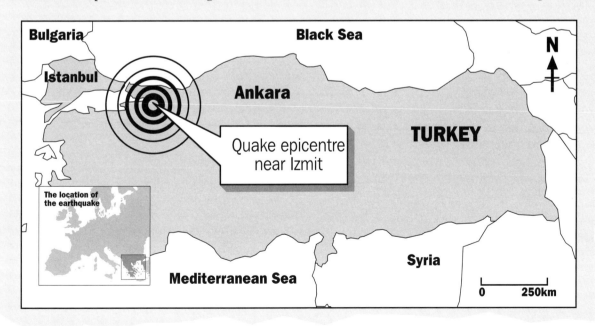

Continued...

Resource 1   *Continued...*

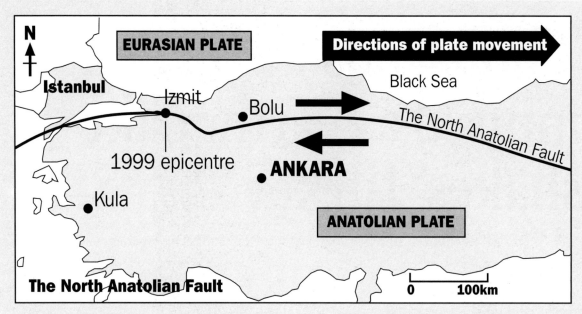

building in Istanbul's Avcilar district. Authorities said at least 156 were killed in Istanbul alone.

Thousands of buildings collapsed in the worst-hit cities and towns. Ahmet Cafoglu, head of the Turkish Standards Institute, blamed shoddy construction for the vast damage and huge loss of life. Roads were severely damaged throughout the region. The energy ministry said two gas-fired power plants were damaged as well as several power transmission lines. There were blackouts in parts of western Anatolia, including Istanbul. Water service was also cut in Istanbul, a crowded city of 12 million people, and other towns.

In Izmit, overwhelmed hospitals were treating people on the pavement. Medical workers broke windows of pharmacies in a desperate attempt to get supplies for hospitals. Tanks at a nearby oil refinery caught fire and have been left to burn out.

The Prime Minister Mr Ecevit thanked foreign countries for offers of aid but warned them of the scale of the disaster and its devastating impact on transport and communications.

France, Germany and Switzerland have dispatched teams of rescue workers and sniffer dogs, along with tons of equipment.

Iran and Israel also offered help. The US agency for international development was dispatching a search-and-rescue advisory team from Fairfax, Virginia, and Miami to provide help in digging out survivors from the rubble. US assistance from military bases in Turkey have offered helicopters, tents and blankets.

Their rescue teams are expected to arrive tonight but will have difficulty in getting to the disaster areas. Turkey says it can shelter and feed the thousands of homeless but asked for specialist teams with sniffer dogs that can find and rescue those trapped under the rubble. Mr Ecevit asked rescuers not to use bulldozers to clear the wreckage, because it might kill those trapped in fragile air pockets.

More than 250 aftershocks followed and Authorities warned people to stay out of damaged buildings, even if the damage seemed minor.

The epicentre was about 45 miles (70 kilometres) southeast of Istanbul, and about 35 miles (50 kilometres) north of Bursa. The quake had a magnitude of 7.8, which made it nearly as powerful as the San Francisco quake of 1906 that destroyed the city.

Tuesday August 17, 1999

Earthquake Damage in Turkey

Resource 3

Magnitude of earthquake	**Location of epicentre**
Building design and construction	**Public awareness and preparedness**
Time (of day, day of week, time of year)	**Loss of life and injuries**
Emergency services	**Relief / geology**
Wealth of people / country	

Demonstrator explanation links

Shock waves will usually weaken with distance from epicentre. Settlements near the epicentre are likely to suffer more damage than distant places.

People might not know what to do. If they run outside they could be hit by falling masonry and glass but they may be safer under a table or in a doorway. Rich countries can tell people what to do through leaflets, TV and at school better than poor countries can.

Rich countries can afford safer designs and better materials to make buildings more earthquake-proof than in poorer countries, so they would be less likely to collapse.

The Decline of Deep Mining on the Northumberland and Durham Coalfield.

Context

This Exemplar was originally developed for Y11 GCSE classes as a component of a unit that combined key ideas of industrial change with those of the impact of human activity on the landscape, supported by Chapter 10: *Industrial Decline and Change* in Rockett et al, (1997). Since then, in a simplified form, it has been used with Y9 classes in a unit on the changing energy industry in the North-East of England. This fits in nicely with and adds a thinking skills dimension to the QCA KS3 Unit 22, *Mining on the Internet.* (QCA, 2000)

The experience of using it with older pupils in a 40 minute lesson with a mixed ability class is described here.

The decline of deep coal mining has multiple causes and given the long history of mining in the area some are quite well understood by the pupils of whom a good proportion have an ex-miner somewhere in the family. The wheel from the last pit's headgear stands outside the Council offices as a reminder of the town's former 'glory'. In the past, pupils had proven themselves more or less able to commit to memory the list of factors responsible for the decline and regurgitate it in exams in much the same format.

Of the list, it occurred to me that only the physical exhaustion of the seams was an independent factor. The others were conditional upon inter-relationships between factors. Lack of investment in modern machinery, for example, had its own causes and effects and impinged upon the costs of extraction. Meanwhile the market price for coal had been influenced by the cheapness of imports, alternatives to coal, the privatisation of power generation and so on. This is a heady brew of interconnected concepts. How were pupils to make sense of it all? How would they begin to organise their understanding into coherently reasoned explanations? Responses to the question in 'mock' exams of previous years on this topic showed that they obviously 'knew' their stuff, but usually failed to make explicit the way certain factors worked together to contribute to decline. Using **Concept Maps** was a way of encouraging better quality explanations.

This particular example has the added element of including ideas that, on the face of it, might have ensured the industry's survival (mechanisation and increasing output per man shift). This is intended to lead to an understanding that change is the result of a balance of forces, not all-or-nothing.

Preparation

In order to encourage thinking about how the factors on the slips are variables, several of the factors are given without saying in which direction they are exerting their influence. So, for example, we have 'North Sea gas' without indicating how it compares with coal in cost terms or whether or not it too is running out. The teacher needs to judge whether or not to add the word 'cheaper' or 'cleaner' to such terms in relation to pupils' prior knowledge. The greater this is, the less detail is required.

You can also decide whether or not to include factors such as Government policy, privatisation, or global warming, or remove some in the light of the age and ability of your classes. In other words, as a strategy, progression can easily be built in by varying the number and sophistication of the factors.

The last deep mine in Northumberland at Ellington had been in the news quite a bit because of concerns that if RJB Mining could not find a buyer, or the Government would not come up with a subsidy, the pit would close. I had recorded a video clip from '*Look North*' about the anxiety of the miners and their families over the possibility of closure. On its own the newspaper cutting would do but without the empathy dimension some of the human cost might be less well appreciated. (*Resource 4*) Pupils were already familiar with the factual aspects of decline: falling employment, falling production, fewer but bigger pits, increasing output per man and the coastwise shift in location over time and so on.

> A characteristic of *TTG* activities is their accessibility and flexibility of use across the age and ability range.

> There are many instances in the geography curriculum where such complex combinations of factors are at work that oversimplification can lead to misconceptions. **Mysteries** in *TTG* are particularly good at exploring the interplay of (often abstract) factors in farming, industrial and urban change. It would be quite straightforward to design one for this topic too.

> This is one approach to further differentiating this Exemplar. However, the more detail that is added, the less thinking there is about the characteristics of the factors.

The only other preparation needed was to arrange seating for groups and provide each with:

- multiple copies of the Guardian article *Aid for Coal Industry on the Way* (*Resource 4*)
- a set of factor cards (*Resource 5 cut into pieces*)
- a sheet of sugar paper
- a lump of blu-tack no bigger than an average conker
- a fine felt pen (although ordinary pens are fine if the paper is light coloured)

Launching

'I burnt the toast this morning. Any guesses why?' By Y11 my classes are quite tolerant of such oblique starts! Someone asked if we were doing a **Mystery**, but I said that there was no mystery to it. The variety of possible causes they came up with was wide: bathroom door jammed, busy marking their homework at the last minute (ha ha!), bread too dry (an interesting line of thought), distracted by Breakfast TV and so on.

Then someone asked *'Electric toaster or grill of the cooker?'* *'Do you think that is significant?'* I asked. He reasoned that if it were a pop-up toaster, there was probably something wrong with it whereas if it were gas it was more likely to be something wrong with me, or words to that effect. I explained that the toaster was broken and that's why I was using the gas cooker. There followed some interesting reasoning and generation of a number of plausible scenarios rich in causes and consequences. I homed in on the one with the most complex set of coincidental factors (eg, no clothes on, postman rings, dog runs out of door into street......) We discussed briefly how events often have multiple causes that themselves may be linked. I connected this to the task in hand by saying that apart perhaps from the coal genuinely all being mined out, it was possibly the case that on their own, the factors in the envelope would not have caused pits to close, but together, they did - and that was what we were going to explore.

Instructions

1. Read through the newspaper article and pose a question like: *'Why is the coal industry today so small and in such a mess?'* Brainstorm the class's ideas.
2. Explain that each of the things they have mentioned is a factor that has influenced the industry, and that these plus a few others they might not have thought about are printed on slips of paper in the envelope.
3. Tell them to open the envelope, spread the factor slips out and see if they can identify any groupings of factors that have strong links with each other.
4. Ask if any would make good headings for the groups.
5. Tell them to write 'PIT CLOSURES' in the middle of the sugar paper and to Blu-tack their chosen headings in the spaces around it.
6. The next step is to arrange the related factors around those headings, link any with drawn lines that they think are related.
7. Write along the line *how* they are connected.
8. Add any other factors to the blank slip and use it where appropriate if they can think of other contributory factors.
9. Tell them not to panic if they can't find a use for them all.
10. Remind them that each factor may have several links.

Managing the activity

Pupils have a compulsion to peek inside the envelopes or start fiddling with the pens so it is important to kick off briskly and get to the activity quickly.

Offer to explain any of the factors that they don't understand. One of the groups comprised well-motivated strugglers and I sat with them to help them get started. I asked them if they knew anyone with a coal fire. One said his nana (grandmother) did have but she'd got gas now. Another said he had a fire that looked like one, but it was really gas. I asked if they thought that might have anything to do with closure of the local pit (its grassy, drumlin-shaped hill being visible out of the window). They said that all the houses they knew of had got gas central heating now and they probably couldn't sell the coal any more. *'Find two slips that you could write that 'story' in between'*. And they were off.

Wacky lines of thinking are not the preserves of the pupils!

Classification is one of the Big Concepts, which, being an information processing device addresses NCTS.

This is a delightful scaffolding episode that takes pupils from the specific to the general and from the familiar to the unfamiliar.

It was plain sailing after they got underway. Those groups that dried up early, I visited to see the quality and quantity of links they had found. *'Expand on this'*, *'Can you think of a reason why these two things be connected?'* would be typical comments. Blank slips are also an invitation to call upon wider knowledge of the issues to introduce factors that we may not have thought about. One group, having heard tell of a grandfather who had bitter memories of the miners' strike thought that might have something to do with it and wrote it on a blank slip. Another group made good use of the newspaper article to explore the relationship between Government and industry.

Circulation is important in this activity to keep encouraging the development of the explanations. Often all that is needed is for you to read one of their briefer explanations and follow it with '*…because?*'.

Debriefing
This focused on a discussion on how this activity might help them write better explanations and some interesting points emerged including:

- it could help you organise your ideas into logical sequences;
- it makes you look for links that you might not think of at first;
- you can see that some factors are more important than others;
- there must be other reasons we don't know or understand behind the ones we do. For example, one group 'knew' that the Government 'hated' the miners, but didn't know why.
- Speculation sometimes gets results. I tend to ask *'Why might…?'* rather than *'Why did…?'* deliberately to encourage this and remove some of the fear of getting something 'wrong'. There is satisfaction from having thought something out for yourself.

Follow-up
For the remaining ten minutes of the lesson, I asked the groups to draft an explanation for the decline of the mining industry beginning with the phrase; 'The reasons why coal mining declined in the North-East are not as simple as they appear because…' (Try this in other contexts too!)

For the less able group it is a good idea to provide a writing frame such as:
*There are……main reasons why mining declined. The first reason is…… and so on.
The first reason occurred because…… and this meant that …… and so on with an encouragement to include words like because, therefore and so that.*

Another valuable way to extend thinking is to discuss **winners and losers** by posing some 'What if…?' question eg:

What if:	Winners	Losers
The Government pays subsidies		
Foreign Governments remove subsidies		
Engineers develop 'clean burn' coal fired power stations		
Some pits close but others stay open		

And before you know it, you are addressing a sizeable chunk of National Curriculum Citizenship at KS4 (DfEE, 1999, p15).

This activity confronts some strongly held opinions in some homes that pit closures were Mrs Thatcher's fault or conversely the result of militancy of the miners. This is cognitive conflict in action.

Teachers' questioning styles change in TT lessons. There are fewer closed recall questions and more that are open and speculative, with reasoning at their core. Watch 'Duncan' teach a **Mystery** lesson on the National Literacy Strategy KS3 videotape.

This is an example of predicting based upon what pupils know and understand of the relationships they have been exploring. This is higher order thinking.

Resource 4

North-East Echo - 16 November, 1999

Coal Industry Profit Warning

The British coal industry moved further into crisis yesterday when RJB Mining, the country's biggest deep mined and open-cast coal producer, issued a profit warning. RJB, which took over most of the pits in England from British Coal in 1994, is now predicting profits of less than a quarter of last year's figure.

RJB has been struggling to compete against foreign imports while its main customers, the British electricity companies, have been turning to other forms of fuel, in particular, natural gas which produces fewer green-house gases.

The high value of the pound makes British coal too expensive to sell abroad and foreign coal cheaper to import. British coal costs on average about £28 a tonne to produce compared with as little as $6 in similar mines in the US.

RJB, which controls more than 60% of coal production in Britain, is reported to be in talks with an Italian businessman about the sale of Ellington colliery in Northumberland which is expected to close in February if a buyer is not found. Ellington is the last operating pit in the north-east coalfield.

North-East Echo - 6 April, 2000

Government Lifeline for Coal Industry

A £70m Government plan to save Britain's ailing coal industry from closure has been proposed following RJB's reported loss of £130m up to last December, compared with a £40.1m profit in 1998.

The Government and the mine owners are awaiting a decision by the European Commission in Brussels to grant permission to subsidise the industry.

Miners' trade union leaders and RJB executives have warned against Britain becoming over dependent

on gas and nuclear power. RJB claims that its 13 deep mines ran at a third of the cost of German collieries, and a fifth of those in Italy, both of which receive substantial subsidies from their Governments.

Mr Budge of RJB Mining said, "It would be ridiculous to be losing UK jobs when European Governments are subsidising theirs." The company has promised to keep all its 13 pits open if its demands for aid are met in full. If not it will close Ellington colliery in the north-east.

The Decline of Deep Coal Mining

Demand for coal	**Alternative sources of energy**
Coal reserves (How much coal is left underground?)	**Cost of coal**
Impact on environment	**Mechanisation**
Increased output per man / shift	**Geology**
Labour costs (Miners' earnings)	**Availability of cheaper coal from overseas**
Investment in new machinery	**Decline of heavy industries**
Dangerous work	**Government subsidies**

Exemplar 3

The Three Gorges Dam - Disaster or An End to Disaster?

Context

The impact of human intervention in natural systems and the social and economic changes that they bring about are meat and drink to the geography curriculum. Dam projects are particularly good for bringing into focus competing arguments and viewpoints and consequently make for good decision-making exercises. They also encourage consideration of short, medium and long term impacts at scales from local to, in this case, global. This Exemplar could be tailored to suit units on energy, managing landform systems, development or hazards but given this versatility, it lends itself to a synoptic study. The Y12 class had a good knowledge of river systems and basin management strategies but development issues and tropical agriculture, for example, were still based on GCSE work.

This Exemplar began life as an A Level exercise for a 40 minute lesson about a month before the summer module exams in Y12. Half the group of 12 would be responsible for constructing the case for the Three Gorges Dam reservoir upstream of Yichang on the Yangtze River in China and the other half against it. I had decided this in preference to adopting particular representative roles such as 'an industrialist', 'a farmer' etc, as I wanted to ensure there was plenty of collaboration in the groups. Their brief included an instruction to anticipate the other side's arguments and in order to understand the various issues we decided to use a **Concept Map.** The group had come across them several times before and I took a chance and gave them the responsibility of identifying between 10 and 15 factors (or concepts) to go on the slips. They seemed to like the idea that they were involved in developing the activity to be used with other students in the future! The result, with only minor tinkering by me to take out some factual details to refine the concepts, is given here. You should consider using these unless your class has some experience of identifying concepts or factors for themselves (*Resource 6*).

Preparation

The news report (*Resource 7*) based on articles in *The China Daily*, brings the scale of the Yangtze flood hazard into sharp focus with details of the July 2000 disaster. These were photocopied. Our core text (Guiness and Nagel, 1999) pp236-237 was used as a resource.

Although not aimed at A Level students, programme two of the Channel 4 series *Changing China: The Three Gorges Project* is an excellent introduction to the issues. Interviews with people affected by flooding helps to engage the emotions and there is plenty of 'awe and wonder' stimulated by such dramatic landscapes and processes. However, environmental issues need to be seen in the context of 10% year on year economic growth, especially industrial, the energy demands associated with it and the ever-growing population. There are numerous sources available on China's economic miracle which could also be provided as resources and an atlas with climate data should be available for reference and to fix the topic spatially. If using this activity with AS or A Level students, *Geo-factfile 110* is a particularly informative resource.

The materials needed were as for the other two Exemplars except that I gave them a dozen blank pieces of paper from a note block on which to write the concepts they thought had parts to play in the arguments for and against the dam. If you prefer to use the concepts in *Resource 6* print a copy for each group, cut them up and put each set in an envelope.

Launching

I began by asking them to recall what they had learned about the Aswan Dam during their GSCE course and there was a pleasing response. They could certainly remember why it had been built and many of its economic, social and environmental effects. Although they had forgotten about the significance to downstream farmers of the trapping of silt in Lake Nasser. I said that this case study contained many similar ideas but a number of additional ones to consider as well. If or when completed it would be the biggest dam in the world. They already knew the objective of the lesson and the role of the **Concept Map** exercise.

Issues such as this are closely associated to the Big Concept of Planning. It is crucial for pupils to grow to appreciate that decisions shape geography and the future state of the world.

Autonomous learners can, of course, design their own meaningful tasks.

It is generally the case that the more the senses and emotions are engaged, the more powerful will be the learning experience.

Published by Curriculum Press, The Big Peg, Vyse Street, Birmingham Tel: 0121 248 3510

This is the activation of prior knowledge. It encourages transfer.

More Thinking Through Geography

Instructions

1 Get them into groups of 3 or 4.

2 Give out the news item (*Resource 7*) to read for a few minutes.

3 Speculate on what alternatives to dam building there may be.

4 Watch *The Three Gorges Dam* video noting down topics ('factors') that might be important to the argument for and against the dam.

5 After the video, ask them to identify and jot down the factors that need to be considered when arguing for or against the dam. Keep them to no more than four words in length or they start to say 'too much'. Write them on the blank slips.

6 Spread the concept slips around the sugar paper and stick them down.

7 Link up related concepts and explain the nature of the relationship along the line.

Managing the activity

All was well until the groups began to discuss what to put on the slips. Discussion boiled down to what the difference was between a fact, a factor and a concept so I intervened to say that they should put down 'things you would need to consider' if they were the decision-makers and this helped. They soon became thirsty for more data so I directed them to the chapter in the textbook and the atlas.

The lesson flew past and we lost sight of the intended debate. In the end we agreed to spend more time exploring the case study and individually to write up notes in response to the title of this Exemplar. To me, the important thing was to have explored and exercised the arguments in discussion. One of the girls questioned if there were enough people nearby to use so much electricity and anyway if people were so poor, what would they use it for? Another raised the matter of farmers needing rich silt to nourish the fields. One boy wondered why flooding matters when farmers flood the fields in the first place. These kind of comments indicated to me that they were questioning assumptions (eg, that all flooding is bad) and actively seeking new understandings.

I could hear during the group work phase that thoughts had roamed far and wide, so I suggested that to organise their notes they should sketch out their ideas in the tabular form below. It was clear to me that they were well able to classify concepts by theme (agriculture, settlements, communications, etc.) but needed some guidance to consider the dam and its consequences at different areal and time scales.

	Short	Medium	Long
Local			
Regional/national			
Global			

You could just as easily build a matrix of social / environmental / economic with either of the above axes.

Debriefing

This was cut short by the end of the lesson but I was interested to know how they had arrived at the words (concepts) on the slips. The group did agree that it was hard to control the number of concepts, that each new bit of information they came across seemed to generate a new one! A group of girls had tackled this problem in effect by carrying out a mini classification exercise (see *TTG* **Classification**) for example, by grouping deaths, food destruction and property damage as '*flood risk*'.

Afterthoughts

I assumed, wrongly, that having used **Concept Maps** before, they would automatically be able to identify concepts on their own. In fact they really needed some exemplification to clarify what was wanted.

With a little alteration it could be used for other major dam schemes and with younger pupils.

With post-16 pupils, it could be combined with a pupil web-search (try searching for *Three Gorges Dam China*) which produces many sites that address the factors more or less directly, though they should be warned away from those with flowery language!

Although in geography we often use these terms interchangeably, there is no consistency of interpretation across the disciplines. There have been some heated debates during mixed discipline INSET sessions that have blown them off course!

It is the mark of a successful TT lesson that pupils have been stimulated to ask questions of their own volition. Here they are clearly exploring the relationships between economic and natural systems.

A scaffolding strategy.

It is to be expected that pupils with some years of TT experience will seek to make use of strategies they have used before and as a result of debriefing, have the confidence to apply them to new contexts. That is the whole purpose of teaching thinking.

Resource 6   The Three Gorges

Flood risk	**Migration**
Fishing	**Agriculture**
Industrial development	**Electricity**
Monsoon climate	**Siltation**
Transport & communications	**Population growth**
Cost	**Tourism**
Global warming	

China Reporter 21.7.2000

Three provinces declare Yangtze state of emergency as 250 lives lost

China Reporter 21.7.2000

Water still rising

Three of China's eastern provinces declared a state of emergency yesterday as flood waters continued to rise above danger levels and threaten provinces along the middle and lower reaches of the Yangtze River.

Emergency powers

Under the Flood Control Law, local flood-control headquarters can remove obstacles from roads and bridges, mobilize materials, vehicles and labour, take control of communications facilities and distribute flood-relief materials.

China Reporter 21.7.2000

Worst yet to come

Flooding on the middle reaches of the Yangtze is becoming more serious in flood-stricken provinces of Jiangxi, Hubei and Hunan, as the water levels in some sections of the Yangtze have exceeded the danger limit for 20 days following heavy rains in late June.

According to the Yangtze River Water Conservation Committee, the biggest flood peak of the season so far was expected to reach Yichang yesterday afternoon, bringing the local water level to an estimated 53.3 metres. The peak is expected to hit Wuhan on Friday.

China Reporter 21.7.2000

Evacuation

The lives of 60 million local residents, more than the entire population of the United Kingdom, are at risk and about 1.84 million people have already been evacuated.

So far 3.5 million hectares of farm land are inundated with 660,000 hectares of crops destroyed. Around 2 million houses have been lost or seriously damaged. Damage so far is estimated to be valued at £2.4 billion.

By 8am yesterday, 20,000 residents of the Paizhouwan Flood Diversion Zone in Hubei had been evacuated to safety in preparation for a possible diversion of flood waters. The authorities plan to remove 57,000 residents from the zone in Jiayu County to protect major cities on the lower reaches of the Yangtze as the flood peak travels down river.

This echoes the point made in the Introduction, that *TTG* strategies are about improving performance. Most can be used for assessment informally and, as in this case, formally.

Assessment

If understanding depends upon being able to develop a web of interconnections which relate knowledge and experience to new ideas being represented then **Concept Maps** can be visible expressions of pupils' understanding. True, they may not show *all* that they understand, but neither do they in question and answer sessions, comprehension exercises or tests! Ultimately, in examinations, if they don't explicitly express their understanding, they don't get the marks. Pupils do need to be reminded frequently to annotate the reasons for the links so that in your mind you could be saying *'This relates to; this causes that; this influences that, because...'*

Looking at pupils', work you quickly realise why you can't evaluate the extent of their understanding by simply counting the links that they have labelled. There will be significant qualitative differences between them in terms of degree of generality, abstractness, and conditionality. The table in *Resource 8* should help you to pick out these qualitative differences and how they can relate to NC Levels. You could just as easily assign mark ranges to them.

Criteria for Assessment

Resource 8

Assessment criteria for this task	Links with Level descriptions
The linkages are based on simple, descriptive relationships, using the form X is/needs Y. Some of the links may be erroneous or inappropriate and lack depth or detail. In most cases a relatively small number of links will have been made.	Pupils are likely to show evidence of attainment characteristic of **Level 4**. They are beginning to describe geographical patterns. They also recognise and describe physical and human processes.
The descriptive facts are adequate but not detailed. The linkages show understanding, but tend to be expressed as simple relationships with words like **is**, **means** and **to** used as connectors, eg: *Quick response means more lives are saved, not enough money to buy ways of communicating.* Increased use of the link **because** indicates an increasing concern with explanation, eg: *Many people died because weak buildings collapsed.* Although all factors might be expected to have one link, an increasing number of linkages, to the point where many have two or more, indicates a greater depth of understanding of the impact of earthquakes.	Pupils' work at **Level 5** is characterised by pupils describing and beginning to offer explanations for a range of physical and human processes. Performance characteristic of **Level 6** includes the explanation of a range of physical and human processes. They recognise interactions between processes.
The descriptive facts are more detailed and include locational and more specific detail. The linkages indicate more sophisticated multiple relationships, eg: *As people have a good amount of money, good buildings can be built and not many will fall down.* Speculation, eg: *If they knew where was worst affected they would go there first.* and qualification of statements, eg: *Thanks to good planning and strong buildings, not many people were killed, although many were injured.*	Pupils' work may show some of the characteristic features of **Levels 7** and **8.** Pupils' work at **Level 7** includes **description** of the interactions within and between physical and human processes. Their work also shows how these interactions create geographical patterns. Where pupils also offer **explanations** for interactions within and between physical and human processes, their work shows attributes more characteristic of **Level 8**. They recognise the causes and consequences of **(environmental)** issues.
Complex multiple interactions are explained. Details are incorporated into explanations and may include ideas imported from personal experience and/or prior knowledge and through inference, eg: *Shanty houses are often built of poor quality materials by people on low incomes and buildings won't comply with building regulations. They are likely to be built on the poorest quality land which may be too steep and prone to landslides as some are around Mexico City, or too flat and likely to flood if dams burst as they might in Northern India.*	**Exceptional performance** is indicated by pupils' work that explains complex interactions within and between human and physical processes, perhaps involving a number of factors simultaneously. They use a wide range of factors to explain and predict change over time (ie causes and consequences).

After SCAA, 1996

Concept Maps are a useful diagnostic assessment tool because they can readily inform you, the teacher, of which elements of conceptual understanding are missing or misunderstood. You can then go through the ideas at the end of the lesson or structure the next lesson to visit them again.

More Thinking Through Geography

Chapter 9

Predicting
with Video

9 Predicting with Video

Rationale

The 'What happened next?' round of A *Question of Sport* is very entertaining not least because it is accessible to all viewers whether it is their favorite sport or one that they are not familiar with. Some prior knowledge of the sport helps to narrow down the possibilities but essentially the viewer studies a sequence of events and based on their understanding of these events through their powers of observation predicts possible outcomes. Prediction can be a very powerful tool in the geography classroom as well.

Geography is awash with visual imagery as are pupils' lives outside school. We cannot assume that they know how to make sense of what they see. In the same way that literacy is more than simply being able to recognise words, visual literacy is about understanding *how to 'read'* (ie question, analyse and interpret) images, in this case *moving images*. Tele-visual resources are hugely valuable secondary sources of evidence that pupils should be taught to use. (NC KS3 2d) But to do this effectively we must teach them to look and listen critically, to make connections between what they already know and what they see and to speculate and hypothesise.

Videos, whether made from public service broadcasts or commercially produced, have identifiable components. Though not necessarily in this order: they establish contexts; identify and explain processes, problems or issues; they consider responses; and finally, they discuss consequences or evaluate alternatives. There is also specific geographical content to these phases, the predictive value of which may be better understood by reference to some of the Big Concepts such as inequality or cause and effect.

Videos can be both over- ('Not *another* video, Sir!') and under-used (What are we watching this *for*, Miss?). Pupils' learning, and indeed their enjoyment, may be obstructed by so many questions that they miss much of the imagery and rely on the soundtrack. They can be easily bored by task repetition and bored just as much by passivity. Pupils should be *actively* engaged in watching the video.

Predicting with Video is a strategy which exploits the visual and auditory learning styles preferred by many pupils. It is not a guessing game but a serious cognitive challenge. In these lessons pupils are shown a carefully chosen video sequence and they have to predict what will happen next based on what has been seen and heard, known and understood, and what understanding and experience the pupils bring with them. This can stimulate a great deal of discussion, and the possibilities for exploration of the relationship between factors at work can be explored in **follow-up** or **debriefing**. Predictions need to be *justified* and therefore pupils are involved in applying their understanding:

- Pupils are actively engaged in watching and listening as opposed to seeing and hearing. Rather than being passive note-takers, they are watching video critically and with a known purpose.

- Predicting involves pupils in gathering evidence, organising it into logical sequences of events, and extrapolating. Sequencing is a higher order thinking skill (Fisher, 1990).

- As a strategy it is closely associated with *cause and effect*, one of geography's Big Concepts.

- It appeals to a large number of students as neither reading nor writing is the main process or outcome.

- **Predicting with Video** is a form of geographical enquiry (Butt, 1991).

- As a group activity it takes advantage of the differing visual and auditory skills and memories of individuals and the sharing of existing knowledge.

Even if you don't have these particular video programmes in your library, you will have plenty of others with which the strategy can be used.

TTG can make a substantial contribution to Citizenship, not least in the area of analysing topical issues presented through visual media.

Using hypotheses to predict, assess trends and evidence to make judgements are specified skills in many GCSE syllabuses.

Migration in North East Brazil

Video: Drought on the Land (BBC Brazil series)

Context

It may well have been made around the time colour TV was invented, but for its ability to convey a sense of place, tap the emotions and to set migration factors within the context of real lives, *Drought on the Land - The Caatinga* in the BBC Brazil series remains a classic. The issues it explores are timeless; the dilemmas highly personalised yet easy to generalise; the choices hard and uncertain; the environment harsh and merciless. You can almost feel the heat coming out of the screen. Like the others in the series but unlike the '2000' series, the programme has a number of really strong story lines which focus on people's lives and each one leaves you with a big, unspoken question hanging in the air: 'What does the future hold?'

I use this programme in a unit on Population (KS3 NC geography 6f with a sprinkling of 6g and 6i). After a fortnight of studying urban patterns and processes in Sao Paulo, including shanty towns and how they grow and mature, the focus shifts to investigate push and pull factors at work in rural Brazil.

All the Y9 classes have had a go at **Predicting with Video**. They are setted by the maths department but they are pretty mixed ability as far as geography is concerned. The group of least able pupils really got a lot out of it. Some of their literacy levels are very low and they responded well when they realised there was not going to be a vast quantity of writing! As a strategy, it really is accessible to the full ability range. This Exemplar describes how it went with a middle of the road class that would sit and watch videos all day if they were allowed to.

> The **Storytelling** strategy in *TTG* makes a strong case for the power of narrative.

Preparation

You really do need to know the structure of the programme well, and a chapter in a book is not an ideal way to explain it! Many programmes produced specifically for secondary education run for 20 minutes which is ideal for a 40 minute lesson though it doesn't leave much time for debriefing. Timings given here are approximate and for your own preparation you should zero the video player counter at the start of the titles. Use the player that you are likely to use in class as the counters can vary from machine to machine. Make sure you know its habits:

- how much unpleasant flicker there is on the screen in 'pause' mode;
- how long it can hold 'pause' before switching itself off;
- how far it winds back when you stop it.

More and more pupils have wide screen TV and surround sound in their living rooms at home. They are not going to be motivated to watch and listen intently if 30 pupils have to crowd round a 14-inch portable perched on a chair on top of a desk, so make sure the viewing conditions are appropriate.

Even if you don't have a copy of this particular video, what follows will give you a flavour of the strategy and perhaps provide some ideas for using other programmes with migration or other themes.

I prepared frameworks for them to jot down their ideas for use in group discussions (*Resource 1*).

Launching

I began with a particularly gruesome idea to capture their attention and it seemed to work. '*Suppose*', I said, '*that you were gazing out of the window as you do when I'm being especially boring and you saw someone fall past. Could you predict what would be the next thing to happen to that person?*' Once Superman and Buzz Lightyear had been set aside, they agreed that they would more than likely be killed when they hit the ground. '*How do you know?*' I asked. Assorted responses to do with gravity, too fast to stop, nothing outside to catch the body and so on were volunteered and we agreed that together these ideas were *evidence*, some of which they had seen (eg, speed of fall), some were drawing on things they already knew (eg, that the wall outside was vertical and free of obstructions) and some they didn't know for a fact, but could work out as being highly likely (the impact would probably kill the person).

> Another example of a lesson's start to set a tone that looks beyond the context of geography in textbook and exams. The effort all the time is to make connections.

We explored what the causes might be for someone falling past the window: suicide; murder; and accident. We'd need more evidence to say. So, we had quickly reached an understanding that with enough evidence we could work out both what had happened and what was likely to happen. If we knew how things worked (in this case, gravity) we could be pretty certain of what happened next or 'prediction'. (You could mention here that newspaper horoscopes are bound to be woolly and inaccurate because the astrologer doesn't have enough evidence about you individually to predict your future!)

I reminded them of the previous lesson in which we had discovered that shanty dwellers were actually from three different sources: migrants; people born there; and people from other parts of the city. I explained that the object of today's lesson was to find out why people in rural areas might decide to migrate to a city and that we would be collecting evidence that would help explain this. I 'predicted' that by the end of the lesson they would have learned about what the rural environment and life in the countryside can be like and what might encourage them to stay or leave.

Instructions
1 Divide each table of four pupils into 'A's and 'B's in preparation for some of the tasks.
2 Tell them to get into positions where they can see the screen clearly and have their notes sheet in front of them.
3 Explain that there is one overarching prediction for the whole programme: Will the eldest daughter of the family, Carmina da Silva migrate to the city or not, and why?
4 Explain that they will see segments of the video during which they should look (or look and listen) for evidence to help predict the 'answers' to the 'questions' on their sheet. As a warm up we 'spotted' different environments as they appeared in the opening titles. The sound was turned down in preparation for the first observational task.

Clip 1 from 'Drought on the Land' (title - 4 mins, silent)
The 'A's in each group would look carefully at the landscape while the 'B's look for evidence of what the weather / climate might be. Use as many adjectives as possible.
Prediction: What kind of lifestyle might people living here have and why?
Stop the video. Discuss in tables and jot down the group's ideas. Feed back to the class.
Prediction: How might the shortage of clean water affect family life? Discuss in open class. Rewind and replay this section with the sound turned up. There is some important contextualising information in the soundtrack.
Continue showing the video with sound on which goes on to describe and explain aspects of rural life. Pupils should continue to add notes to the boxes on the *Resource* sheet.

Clip 2 (at 9 mins, sound on)
This describes the traditional relationship between people and the river then introduces the Sobradinho dam scheme on the Sao Francisco River.
Stop the tape.
Predict: What do you think the electricity company did for the people displaced by the reservoir?
The 'A's predict who might be the gainers of the project. The 'B's predict who might be losers. Why?
Discuss in groups and predict whether life would be better or worse for the people who originally lived by the river after the construction of the dam. Feed back to the class.

Clip 3 (13 mins, sound on)
This concerns resettlement schemes in two new towns. Groups review and remodel their ideas from the previous clip and report back briefly.

Clip 4 (17 mins, sound on) Returning to the da Silva family.
'A's concentrate on reasons for Carmina da Silva (the eldest daughter) to want to leave.
'B's focus on why she may want to stay or not be able to leave.
Predictions: 'A's - What might her life be like if she goes to the city?
                   'B's - What might her life be like if she stays?

Discuss this in groups and feed back to the class.
Finally, given the evidence, the class takes a vote on whether or not she migrates to the city.

Existing knowledge is being activated and used to infer meaning.

Very important Information-processing skills (NCTS) are being practised here.

Managing the activity

It is good practice for pupils to know what they are looking and listening for at each stage. I checked that they understood the next task before restarting the tape. Once they did, it was amazing how seriously they paid attention.

The feedback for *Clip 1* was excellent. I asked each table in turn to contribute something to describe the environment and only threw it open when one group dried up. I suggested that they add words to their own notes if they thought them appropriate. These included: barren, desolate, risky, dusty and burnt. Vegetation was described as: thin, hard, inedible, no grass or trees, cactuses and dead-looking. The weather / climate was: burning, tiring, hot, sweaty, like desert.

I resisted the temptation to break the continuity of the programme too much by elaborating at the discussion stages and decided to let the programme 'do the talking'. However, I did discretely monitor their discussions and inserted the occasional question such as *'Do you think the traffic on the road had anything to do with their lives?'* to add new dimensions to group discussions. It was by eavesdropping that I realised that the term 'lifestyle' in the first predicting stage was a bit vague. I had used the word instead of 'making a living' which suggests only economic activity and I wanted them to be thinking about all aspects of life: health issues, access to services, forms of recreation and so on. So I had to explain what I wanted. They came up with words like hard, agricultural, boring, hungry, sick, poor, sad and strong family ties.

The other tasks worked really well. The sense of injustice at the actions of the electricity company had the class buzzing. It wasn't part of my plan, but to take time out to discuss what people with few or no resources could do about such a situation would resonate with some objectives of the citizenship curriculum.

> See Section 1A of
> Citizenship NC

After feed back from 'A's and 'B's predicting what may happen to her if she stays or goes, the final vote decided in favour of Carmina Da Silva migrating to the city though one boy said it should be conditional upon her sending back some of her earnings. *'Well, I wouldn't, if I'd earned it and who's going to stop me going anyway?'* said one of the girls. Someone else said it was unfair that she should get all the advantages. What about all the other kids? Sometimes you just can't keep PSE out of the geography classroom!

Debriefing

There are numerous aspects of this activity that could be debriefed but at the start of the lesson we had discussed the importance of evidence collecting as an aid to prediction. After a brief discussion about how good their predictions had been I asked what kinds of evidence they had used and how they had reached their predictions. As you might expect, they referred to what they had heard and seen but interestingly they said they had 'worked things out'.

> Reasoning skills are at
> work here ie, they 'draw
> inferences and make
> deductions' NCTS.

I decided to explore this 'working out' with the 'lifestyle' task. Initial responses of dirty, poor, horrible, and boring needed fleshing out. With prompts like *'Well if it's hard to keep things clean, what might that lead to?' 'And if you don't feel well…?'*, and *'What do you think it means to live without a power supply?'* one group described their reasoning about the lifestyle of the family, summarised as follows:

> *Polluted pond water means no clean water to drink, dirty clothes, and obviously not enough to water crops, so probably hungry and sick. Cooking on wood stove so no electricity or gas supply, so no fridge to keep food fresh or TV for entertainment. Probably go to bed at sunset. Boys might spend ages fetching wood, because can't see any around. If they don't, can't boil water and will get sick. They won't be able to do much then.*

This was an excellent example of how pupils can generate 'new knowledge' through discussion.

Follow-up

I set them a choice of writing-up tasks to consolidate points made during the lesson, both of which provide the opportunity to incorporate prediction.

Either

Imagine you are one of the farmers shown in the programme and the Minister for Rural Development is coming to visit the Caatinga region. You decide to attend a public meeting in town. Explain to him:

a) the problems you and your family face;

b) what practical help you would like the government to offer;

c) what will be the consequences (short and long-term) if you don't receive help?

or

Imagine you are the Minister for Rural Development and you have visited the Caatinga region and seen at first hand the difficulties people face. You go to a meeting with the Minister of Finance and the Minister for Urban Affairs to argue for a bigger share of Government money to be spent helping the drought zone rather than the cities. What will you say at the meeting to convince them?

Only a few of the more able pupils chose the second option, perhaps because it is less structured, but some highly persuasive writing came out of it.

> The writing was helped by the intrinsic motivation the pupils had generated. Thinking helps writing.

Drought on the Land

Clip 1
A group: Landscape (what the land looks like)
B group: Weather now / weather usually
Predict what kind of lifestyle might people living here have?

Clip 2
Predict what you think the electricity company did for the people displaced by rising reservoir water.
A group: Gainers from the dam project
B group: Losers from the dam project
Review: Would life be better or worse for the people who used to live by the river?

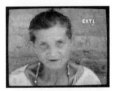

Clip 3
Review and remodel predictions from Clip 2

Clip 4
A group: What might the future hold for Carmina Da Silva if she goes to the city?
B group: What might the future hold for Carmina Da Silva if she stays?

Exemplar 2

Conflict and Change in Urban Areas: Development Processes

Video: The Changing City - London. (*Geographical Eye over Britain*, C4)

Context

I tried this Exemplar in a single period plus homework with my Y12 group of 14 as part of the NEAB A Level unit 'Managing Cities' in September. After the long holiday, I was keen to get their minds back onto the subject.

The class had a few outstandingly able pupils who would lap up anything as long as they could see the point of it. Some others just seemed to want conveyor belt feeding. I wanted to get them interacting with each other and with geographical ideas, but I have to admit that I have struggled to find signs of life sometimes and enthusiasm is an alien concept.

Economic and social changes in cities, however, are not. The class had previously studied the impacts of de-industrialisation in Glasgow and contrasted them with change in Manchester before the summer break.

The aims of this lesson were to understand that:

There is a strong citizenship dimension here. This activity touches strongly on the planning and decision-making process. Cause and effect are important too.

- change benefits some and disadvantages others and therefore causes social conflict;
- change can come about through economic success or decline and through political action;
- the urban planning process considers different views, but arrives at decisions which may over-ride local wishes in the interest of a bigger ideal or more powerful influence.

Like photographs, videos are versatile if the activities associated with them are varied and challenging. This series, *Geographical Eye over Britain* is pitched at GCSE Level but not limited to it. It throws up issues that can be explored with varying degrees of sophistication. '*The Changing City*' looks at causes of urban change and contrasts the very different models of redevelopment that took place in Docklands and Coin Street, Waterloo. Opportunities for predicting are mixed in with more 'normal' activities.

Preparation

I had previously recorded the opening sequences of *Eastenders* with its remote sensing imagery of the Docklands part of the East End of London and some snippets of environment and life around Albert Square. I also had collected some cuttings concerning the controversy over the troubles of the Millennium Dome in Greenwich for a wall display, the intention being to demonstrate that the issues concerned with urban change recur.

So as not to anticipate the process of change at Coin Street, I wound the programme forward to the start of the potted history of the growth of London which begins with a map of England after 2 minutes.

Launching

I began by reminding them of things they had learned in science: anything organic is made of living matter and that living things have life cycles. If they don't reproduce, they die out. In a similar way, cities are 'living organisms'. I showed the clip of *Eastenders* until they had seen the street market and a shot of 'The Vic' pub then asked them to brainstorm how many characters had come and gone that they could remember. Conclusion: the populations of cities are constantly renewing themselves.

I then asked what changes to businesses and employment could they recall (legal and illegal!). These included changes of ownership, a relaunched café and a dodgy car dealership among others. Conclusion: enterprises are continually forming and folding.

More connections are being established here. Pupils are more likely to transfer learning if the boundaries between subjects and between school and life are constantly crossed.

I then tried the first bit of prediction in open class: *What changes to the life and environment of Albert Square might result from a) a supermarket opening and b) an office block going up around the corner?* In 2 minutes we had some excellent ideas: food stalls in the market closing or going elsewhere; influx of middle class executive types; rising property prices; new job opportunities; more traffic congestion – to name a few.

I soft soaped them by saying that they clearly understood the 'organic' nature of change in urban areas. They would now look at how other nearby parts of London have changed, and then predict how change might occur in the future.

Instructions

- Sit them in groups of about 4.
- Get each group to appoint a spokesperson for feeding back ideas to the class.
- Show the sections of the video with sound except the black and white section (3-4 minutes in).

Clip 1

This phase is to establish some of the bases of the need for redevelopment.

1   Give each group one of three tasks:
    - to carefully describe the physical environment;
    - to deduce what the quality of lives of people in the area might be;
    - to work out what local employment opportunities might be and what workplace skills are needed.

2   Each group should speculate (predict) how those aspects of old Docklands have changed.

3   Show the 1 minute clip of the Docklands in the 1930s without sound then give 3 minutes to discuss what they can interpret and infer from the images.

4   Ask the spokesperson for each group to report to the class on their particular theme.

5   (Optional) Rewind and re-run this section with the soundtrack on. Don't bother if their ideas are well formed. (They may not register that all the workers were male, for example)

Clip 2

This describes how Docklands was redeveloped with primarily commercial considerations.

6   Ask them to take particular note of who benefitted and who did not, and how it came to be developed this way.

7   Stop the tape at 7 minutes and clarify the decision making process for this scheme: no public participation.

8   Give them 2 minutes in groups to discuss if they think this is a good or bad way to go about regenerating a derelict part of a city.

9   Identify changes in the skills required in the new jobs market.

Clip 3

This section (7-12 minutes) describes changes to the Waterloo area since World War 2 and the Coin Street residents' resistance to commercial developers.

10 Ask pupils to note down how Coin Street came to be redeveloped the way it did. Repeat Number 8 above.

Clip 4

The remaining minutes show how the achievement of the ideals of the Coin Street scheme have been slowed by financial constraints and how the expansion of arts based developments on the South Bank is beginning to undermine the viability of the community - based scheme.

11 Watch this section. Then, in groups, discuss what might to happen to the Coin Street area in future years. Allow at least five minutes for this.

12 Feed back predictions with reasoning to the class.

Cognitive conflict here plays an important part in helping pupils to see the shades of grey and to begin to appreciate alternative viewpoints.

Managing the activity

The ideas the groups come up with usually depend on how much previous knowledge they can call upon. This class already knew about slum clearance and high rise residential redevelopment schemes and had a predisposition to side with wishes of local residents! On the other hand some had visited Canary Wharf on family trips to London and had come back mightily impressed, so we had plenty to chew on in discussions. We also have smaller scale dock and quayside redevelopment schemes along the Tyne to feed into the debates.

Some pupils see the issues in black and white: either as laissez-faire capitalists or as utopians. If the other groups don't 'attack' them you may have to prompt the consideration of alternative views by posing questions such as *'Where do you think the wealth generated by the offices might go?'* or *'What are the implications for travel and transport of a scheme?'*

I was happy to field questions that came out of the group discussions, some of which I couldn't answer eg, *How were the Coin Street residents able to raise the money to buy such valuable land?* Others indicated some quite sophisticated thinking eg, *Was it the (national) Government or the local Council that made the redevelopment decisions?* It emerged that they couldn't understand why there hadn't been public protests and action in Docklands like there had been at Coin Street.

The groups' predictions for the future of Coin Street were useful for revealing which urban processes they were thinking through. Different groups suggested:

- encroachment of the arts developments eventually triggering off another round of community action;
- local residents cashing in on the spiralling property values and moving away;
- the population was falling anyway and local services were deteriorating so the community would fade away and be replaced by artists and actors.

Nice ideas.

Follow-up

This was a written exercise to evaluate the two contrasting approaches to urban regeneration shown in the video. With the Millennium Dome and its site so much in the news it was a perfect opportunity to add the task of suggesting a *process* for arriving at a development scheme that might satisfy both local and commercial needs. Later, we compared and contrasted Tyneside's answer to the Tate Modern and Millennium bridge: the new, non-wobbling 'blinking eye' bridge and the old flour mill arts centre 'ower the watter' in Gateshead.

Debriefing

I only had time to focus on predicting the future of Coin Street. Here is a snippet from the discussion:

There is an emerging pattern in the thinking. This facilitates transfer.

> **Me:** *What makes a sound prediction?*
>
> **Pupil 1:** *Not really guessing but trying to work out what's likely to happen.*
>
> **Me:** *How?*
>
> **Pupil 1:** *Well, you know what's happened in other places.*
>
> **Me:** *But it was different in each of the cases we've looked at.*
>
> **Pupil 2:** *You're never going to get two exactly the same. There'll be special things like, maybe, a special building people like, they want to keep.*
>
> **Me:** *Or special people, like the man in Coin Street and Amy's mum. Anything else?*
>
> **Pupil 1:** *No, I meant if you know about planning and who's got the money or whatever to make something happen.*
>
> **Me:** *I see. It's the process of change: who's got the power; whose voice is going to be listened to. That's politics and economics.*

I made the point that while the details of case studies are important (for quoting in the exams) if they understand the process of change and can understand what motivates the movers and shakers, they would be able to transfer those ideas to new situations. I can't be sure that they all can put this idea into effect though. For one or two, money-making is the only factor they understand!

Afterthoughts

The Changing City-London contains some graphics of the style used in the urban development simulation game *Sim City*. This is a rather time consuming game but one worth experiencing because the player (in the role of the planning decision-maker) is made to think about development priorities and effects of decisions, including political consequences. Harsh economic realities have to be faced too. You can choose from a range of existing cities with different problems to try your hand at improving. Try getting pairs to be 'the Mayor' in relays during their free study periods. This is not without its risks. Pupils usually do know how to cause social mayhem, set the city on fire or invite an invasion by aliens. However, it's great fun and there are plenty of 'serious' points to be drawn from it.

Exemplar 3	# Coastal Processes

Video: Shifting Coastlines - East Coast (*Geographical Eye over Britain*, C4)

This is a really quick and easy one to illustrate that the strategy can be used with physical geography videos too.

Context

My Y10 mixed ability GCSE class was a nice bunch who were generally happy to try anything, especially if it had video in it! The 40 minute lesson fitted into an enquiry unit called 'Can coastlines be managed?' At the start of the unit it was clear that the thought had never crossed their minds, but discussion about places they'd visited revealed a huge amount of human intervention in coastal systems although I didn't put it in those terms!

The idea of predicting with this video was to engage pupils in thinking about how the processes work.

Preparation

A physical wall map of Britain was put up for locating the Holderness coastline. It isn't essential, but I find a simple demonstration is an attention catching way to start, so a handful of modelling clay was borrowed from the art room and a lump of chalk brought back from a trip to Sussex were put on a school kitchen tray together with a mug of water and an old toothbrush. It helps to have a sink at the side of the room or a damp cloth for washing your hands.

Launching

I gathered the class round the front table, showed them the chalk and clay and established that they do make up some of the land we live on and are therefore geological. I asked them that if I wet the rocks and brushed them, what did they think I'd be demonstrating? They knew it was to do with erosion. I got a pupil to slowly pour water over first one then the other, while I brushed gently as he poured. The clay was 'eroded' very easily, the chalk less so but underneath them were two pools and splashes of red/brown and milky water.

The first prediction was for the class as a whole:

> What would happen if these two kinds of rock occurred where land meets sea?
>
> What kinds of landforms might we see there?

I sent them back to their table groups to jot down ideas.

Instructions

1 Ensure that they can see the TV screen.

2 Show the first $5^1/_2$ mins which explains the erosional process working on Flamborough's chalk and Holderness' boulderclay, then stop the tape.

3 Ask groups what they had expected to be different and why. The main one was that they hadn't thought such soft rocks could form substantial cliffs.

4 Play the tape for the next 30 seconds which describes how groynes work.

5 Time for the next prediction: '*If groynes trap sand moving along the beach, what will be the effects further along the coast?*' Discuss in groups and feed back to the class.

6 Re-start the video which goes on to explain how the lack of beach exposes the clay cliffs to direct wave action. (Audible whispers of 'Told you'!)

> This mini-enquiry builds in NCTS Enquiry skills.

7 Stop the tape when the cliff-top resident crumbles the clay in his hand. Ask groups to suggest ways in addition to groynes that erosion might be controlled. These could be brainstormed if your lesson time is short. Push them to explain *how* each idea would work.

8 Watch to the end of the programme.

Managing the activity

This is only a small deviation from how I often get pupils to interact with video anyway, and as an activity it needs little special managing. What really impressed me was the pupils' concentration, checking their thinking against the explanations of the video.

I was asked to run over how groynes work again which I did on the board.

One slightly irritating feature of the programme is the almost complete absence of appropriate technical terms. Erosion is described rather superficially but there is no mention of attrition or hydraulic action even in the wildest of storms! Tempting though it was to keep stopping the tape to establish the terminology, I decided to leave that until a later text book-based activity.

Debriefing

They said that the hardest part was predicting the effects of the groynes because most pupils had never really considered beaches as having come from anywhere in particular, or that they can go away, or what there is underneath! The easiest challenge had been thinking of other protection measures, because within each group there were enough personal experiences to draw on. One boy said the whole exercise had been too easy. He used to live on the coast. Perhaps I should have found that out beforehand and made better use of him as a resource.

> Having more background knowledge, this boy constructed new understanding more easily than the others did.

One girl said she suddenly realised what the promenade at Whitley Bay was for. The cliffs are so soft near there that you can stick your finger in them, she informed us. Now there's an image to take away from the lesson!

> A case of transfer between locational contexts here.

Follow-up

Apart from the standard diagrams and explanations of coastal processes for the remaining 10 minutes of this lesson and most of the next one, I gave them as a homework, the task of bullet pointing two sets of arguments: *for* and *against* trying to prevent coastal erosion. They did this quite well, I thought. In the next lesson I followed it up by showing the *'Debate'* section of the BBC *Landforms* programme on coasts which presents a range of alternative arguments.

Developing the strategy

The sequencing of ideas underlies higher order thinking and numerous strategies in the *TTG* repertoire either involve it directly (eg, **Mysteries, Mind Movies, Living Graphs, Layered Decision Making, 5W**) or provide stepping stones towards it (eg, **Classification, Concept Maps**). You can build in prediction to almost any geography lesson.

a) Using other televisual resources

Most teachers make use of other broadcast material in their teaching, especially news programmes. Next time there is a disaster or serious weather warning or anything where there will be consequences over several days, record in series the news items daily. Later, in class, you can show the first item and get the class to predict the next day's news, and so on. This is an interesting exercise in media awareness, raises the question 'What happens after the cameras have gone?' and promotes understanding of short, medium and long term effects and responses.

Most feature films are far too long to show in normal lessons but there are some excellent scenes which can form the basis of extended predictions, perhaps involving storyboarding and certainly providing opportunities for developing pupils' literacy. Three quarters of the way through *Medicine Man* for example, a bio-medical research scientist (Sean Connery) meets the road builders in the middle of the Amazon jungle. What a place to stop and get pupils to continue the script and predict the story! A word of caution: showing a whole film is likely to breach copyright laws. LEAs usually have a licence agreement with the Education Recording Agency allowing you to show extracts. Non-LEA maintained schools may have their own agreement.

b) Using digital cameras

Most schools have one somewhere. The mini - screen images in *Resource 1* of *Exemplar 1* were taken by an ordinary digital camera of a TV screen in a dimly lit room then saved in a Word file on a computer. It is easy to adjust most televisions to give black and white pictures but if you can't, either the digital camera itself can do it or you can take the colour out in *Picture Editor*. The results are remarkably good and gain in definition when reduced in size for incorporation in resource sheets.

See **Storytelling** in
TTG p77

They seem to be excellent triggers for remembering the context surrounding the still image and are therefore a help in writing up or as foci for discussions. Most importantly, you can easily make **storyboards** or **points of view** resources where *real* thoughts can be put in speech bubbles from images of characters featured in the video.

The widespread use of video seems to have all but wiped out the use of slide projectors for a range of valid reasons but as a result, pupils rarely have time to dwell on an image, to interrogate it and to understand it without that awful flicker or automatic shut down. Digital camera images offer a solution and open up the possibility of linking the **Reading Photographs** strategy (*TTG*) with **Predicting with Video.**

c) Linking with other TTG strategies
Video resources are valuable stimuli and contributors of both information and understanding. You can easily add a predictive element to the videos used in **Concept Maps** *Exemplars 1* (Earthquakes) *and 3* (Three Gorges Dam) as a means of encouraging pupils to identify key concepts.

Making connections
again. This time
for teachers!

If you aren't already using it, take a look at the excellent QCS KS3 unit 4 *Flood disaster - how do people cope?* Section 3. Pupils are invited to make reasoned predictions about the effects of floods in Bangladesh and this could be done using your own video news clips, Channel 4's *Geographical Eye over Asia* programme 4, *Living with Floods* or the Action Aid video pack *Bangladesh*. Pupils can make use of **Classification** headings established in section 2 of the unit. This strategy is examined in detail in *Chapter 7* of *TTG*.

Chapter 10

Departmental Visions and Planning for Change

10 Departmental Visions and Planning for Change

What is the big educational agenda and who is driving that agenda – Government, LEA, schools, teachers or students?

Good teachers always have the needs of their students at the heart of what they do. These teachers take time to evaluate their work and to consider the best ways in which to develop the students' skills, knowledge and understanding and their ability to learn. There is increasing interest from classroom teachers in the processes by which their students learn. It is important that teachers are able to see that their concern for enabling their students to maximise their potential is at the heart of schools' activities and is also the focus of much of the present plans for transforming teaching and learning. It is also central to the work of the successfully self-evaluating school. A 'big picture' suggesting linkages between current initiatives in education is shown in *Figure 10.1*.

There are essentially two interrelated issues. The first is finding ways of improving standards of achievement in relation to the current National Curriculum, GCSE, A Level and vocational qualifications. The second is a longer term debate to consider the nature of the curriculum itself and its applicability for life in the 21st Century. The two are not separate from one another and good teachers will always ensure that students create their own meaning and make the vital connections between the school curriculum and everyday life.

The current concern to raise standards is central to Government programmes and they have taken a range of

Figure 10.1 - **THE EDUCATION AGENDA BIG PICTURE**		
Key elements of the education scene, January 2000		
Government policy: Transforming teaching and learning, including thinking skills Literacy Numeracy/mathematics ICT Ofsted inspect schools Beacon schools Advanced Skills Teachers	**LEAs and others:** Enact Government policies through monitoring programmes and Standards Fund allocations, eg: Education Development Plans to drive the School Improvement agenda Schools causing concern Excellence in Cities Sharing of good practice Education Action Zones	**Higher Education Institutions (HEI) based research:** Thinking skills, other learning focused initiatives, and pedagogy to shape future curriculum development.
Schools: Set up effective self evaluation mechanisms which identify not only the key issues, but the action plan to address them. Action plan includes Professional Development (PD) plans for teachers.	**Enabling students to maximise their potential**	**Schools interact with HEIs:** To develop research programmes, but also use outcomes of research.
Classroom teachers: Through performance management, teachers identify professional development programmes which address individual as well as whole school needs.	**Students:** Identify their own learning needs and how they learn best.	**Classroom based action research:** To develop and share improved teaching and learning - from teacher to teacher.
NB The boxes are not mutually exclusive - they all link with one another		

actions to raise the status and importance of the debate. They vary from highly funded programmes for all schools to a focus on some schools who have actual and/or relative underachievement. Running parallel to this is a wish to share good practice widely and effectively with an urgency which is at times unreasonable.

There are potential tensions between two situations:
- getting it done by the quickest possible means through well defined potentially mechanistic programmes;
- taking your time, which implies that a generation may miss out on more stimulating and effective ways of learning.

The highly funded programmes such as the National Literacy and Numeracy strategies are dominating the work of primary schools - they are based on a clear philosophical stance about how children learn best. The impact of these programmes is already being recognised by many secondary schools keen to maximise the benefits for their students from Y7 onwards. The approaches being developed for learning literacy and numeracy/mathematics at Key Stages 1, 2 and 3 can undoubtedly promote more effective learning in many curricular areas. Many of these approaches have already been advocated by *TTG*. The QCA schemes of work for geography do begin to recognise the need to address how learning takes place, in particular through the development of units which promote thinking skills. This work is based on classroom based research by the *TTG* group.

The focus on underachievement is coming through the outcomes of Ofsted inspections and LEA monitoring to identify those schools which are less successful in enabling their students to achieve in line with or above their ability. Linked to this are programmes which address disaffection and the impact of social disadvantage (Education Action Zones, Single Regeneration Budget Areas, Excellence in Cities). It is intended that good practice in teaching and learning should be developed and shared through such initiatives as Beacon Schools, Advanced Skills Teachers and Best Practice Research Scholarship programmes which fund the work of those schools and individuals who have been identified as demonstrating good practice.

For the classroom teacher who is trying to provide the best for her/his students this is a potentially bewildering landscape and yet it is fertile ground for their innovative practice. The next few years will see an exponential growth in the sharing of good practice between departments and individual teachers through the use of ICT. The greatest challenge will be to ensure that the work is monitored and evaluated, so the best practice can be shared with a confidence that it really makes a difference.

So what is the importance of thinking skills in all this?
The Geography National Curriculum has been revised twice, but in fact each revision was dependent on the original document. The original was published in 1990, but the discussion of its content pre-dates its publication.

The review published in 1995 was less than the first, but nothing new could be added. The Curriculum for September 2000 is a more flexible revision of this. This matters when one considers that 80% of our knowledge about the human brain and how it learns has been accumulated over the last 15 years. Understanding about the different functions of specific parts of the brain has led to a more sophisticated appreciation of what happens in learning situations.

'Teaching and learning are not coterminous. Energetic and conscientious teaching can produce little or no learning. Similarly learning can take place with little or no teaching.' (Smith, 1999). Recent work on the functionality of the brain provides some clear messages for teachers and this needs planning for in our geography curriculum. We do not need to reject our current geography, but simply to change the focus, in order to incorporate recent research about learning into our planning.

Unfortunately, many teachers attempting to deliver an overcrowded geography curriculum and meet targets have become driven by subject content - concentrating on content, rather than on the tools and mental models that help us to make sense of geographical content, and to transfer it to other contexts. As teachers, we need to be more explicit about how our students learn rather than what they learn, so that they become geographers rather than people who know something about geography.

The National Curriculum for 2000 has started the ball rolling. In the section entitled 'Promoting other aspects of the Curriculum' the NC Order for geography states that the subject provides opportunities to promote:

thinking skills, through emphasis on the process of geographical enquiry, and helping pupils to evaluate information and reflect on their own work.

But until the process of geographical learning is made explicit within all areas of the National Curriculum it is unlikely to affect learning to any great extent - unless teachers choose to take hold of the agenda for themselves.

'Create the future, don't let it just happen'... visions for geographical education
This is from a statement used by the GeoVisions group of the Geographical Association to drive the evolution of geography education.

How might geography departments look beyond the given agenda in order to establish educational visions of their own?

The recent 'top down' model in education has contributed to the erosion of teachers' confidence in their own professionalism in making curriculum judgements and decisions. The lack of ownership has tended to stifle creativity and sap confidence, particularly in relation to assessment for learning in geography. There is a need for leaders in geography to establish a departmental vision which not only recognises the agendas set by the government, LEA, whole school, but also aims to meet the educational needs of their own pupils in preparing them for adult life in the 21st Century - to seize the opportunity to create a *preferred future* rather than the *probable future*. The latter might result from a narrow interpretation of the present educational debate as only being concerned with raising standards in the confines of end of key stage assessments.

In recent years, teachers have often been working to an imposed agenda that has been constantly shifting and so it has been difficult to assimilate and make sense of the 'big picture'. A useful starting point for departments wishing to comprehensively integrate thinking skills and other associated learning initiatives into teaching and learning approaches might be the creation of a shared five year departmental vision. Such a vision is important as it reinstates 'teacher professional judgement' and ensures that young people studying geography in an individual institution have their own particular needs met. Currently, one of the key vehicles for managing change and educational development is the annual development plan, but for many geography departments such a paradigm shift may require longer term planning. Consequently the establishment of a five year strategic plan from which annual development plans and professional development implications emerge may help to shape this potentially lengthy and complex process.

Any such vision for geographical education for the future of your pupils in a school should recognise:

- the starting point in terms of current teacher expertise within the department, resources, existing schemes of work and teaching and learning approaches;

- the specific needs of the students being taught geography in the individual institution eg, ethnic background, SEN, social context, and their roles as citizens in their own communities;

- what geography has to offer young people in terms of knowledge, understanding and skills necessary for lifelong learning and particularly as a preparation for adult life;

- the need for the vision to evolve in response to changing external, school and departmental agendas and as teachers review their perceptions and judgements about learning geography.

So what might such a geography department vision look like?

The development of Thinking Skills should be seen as integral to all aspects of the work of the department. They are not a panacea, but can offer classroom-based solutions to many current issues such as disaffection, literacy and Key Skills development, spiritual, moral, social and cultural education. They offer considerable scope for teachers as members of a profession that seeks to improve itself and its practice through classroom-based research and self-evaluation processes.

Managing departmental change

Thinking Skills might be introduced into a department's curriculum in a variety of ways which might range from their comprehensive integration (as suggested in The Departmental Vision *Figure 10.2*) to a more piecemeal approach. The latter may be more suitable for departments which are still at an awareness raising stage and where expertise is limited and commitment with regard to such learning strategies is cautious. In such instances, the introduction of a range of 'off the peg' activities into existing schemes of work and units of study would provide professional development and offer teachers the opportunity to observe student responses to such approaches. Either way, one of the key tools for the management of such change within a department (and a school) is its development plan. (*Figure 10.3*)

Departmental development plan

In order to be effective and far reaching, the development plan should:

- evolve from and link back to the whole school development plan;

- evolve from and feed back into the five year departmental vision;

- include SMART targets;

- fully acknowledge all individual and departmental training needs as part of professional development, identifying where and when training will take place eg, departmental meetings;

- provide mechanisms for sharing research and positive development outcomes across the department and beyond;

- be evaluated by the whole department at the end of its cycle.

Teacher performance review processes can provide fertile ground for the introduction of, and training in, thinking skills, especially when a 'classroom research' or 'lesson observation' component is introduced.

Lesson observation

It is important to realise that the creation of a supportive learning environment and other approaches geared to promoting more effective learning are as pertinent to the processes of teacher professional development as they are to pupils' learning. Therefore, it follows that staff respond positively to lesson observation where there is:

- peer coaching or mentoring;

- observation tailored to focus on specific, individual needs;

- discussion and consultation at every stage;

- a clear and negotiated purpose and focus for classroom observation agreed by the observed teacher and the observer - this allows effective reflection on practice;

- a manageable number of foci;

- a structured debriefing session between the observer and the observed teacher after lesson observations -

involving reflection, evaluation, target setting, needs analysis, agreed professional development programme, and an agreement on what can be recorded and shared with other audiences.
(See Figure 10.4)

Key outcomes of lesson observation:

- a greater level of reflective discussion about teaching and learning than previously; classroom practice is discussed more openly and critically;
- a greater variety of teaching and learning approaches;
- teachers thinking more about learning objectives and concentrating on making these clear to pupils;
- teachers more willing to share ideas about classroom practice with colleagues;
- more collaboration between departments... greater understanding of what constitutes effective classroom practice across school;
- teachers confident that standards will rise as a result of classroom observation policy.

Increasingly teachers are finding that keeping reflective diaries and getting pupils to make entries in learning logs/diaries can provide additional information which can inform improvement.

Issues surrounding lesson observation:

- the process takes a considerable amount of time to carry out effectively and will place time demands on middle managers especially if they have large departments;
- there are currently few 'thinking skills experts' in individual schools to act as peer mentors and observers;
- not all schools are well positioned geographically to link with HEIs able to support such professional development.

Other considerations:

- To identify programmes of development for thinking skills and other learning initiatives which match with Standards Fund allocations. This may provide schools (and geography departments) with money or access to expertise which can support professional development. These DfEE funded allocations have been greatly increased in recent years in real terms and in the degree of delegation from LEAs.
- Partnership with HEI and other research bodies - as a means to accessing financial support and/or expertise.

What are the potential conflicts and issues surrounding the introduction of thinking skills?

The content versus process debate

Many teachers feel there is a tension between getting through the curriculum content as opposed to spending time engendering quality learning approaches in pupils. Is this just a perceived conflict? Are educators too driven by 'hard' summative assessment outcomes rather than by how young people learn best?

Can pupils' thinking skills be developed using off-the-peg activities or must departments engage in a more fundamental 'root and branch' approach to change? There is an enormous 'feel good factor' generated when teachers are provided with another thinking skills activity to take away with them at teacher training events. *'Just keep the thinking skills activities coming and we'll carry on attending LEA professional development programmes'* (a comment on an LEA course evaluation form). Unfortunately the lack of time, expertise and confidence may work against the evolution of geographical education in the 21st Century because teachers will only feel confident to adopt other peoples' work rather than shape and develop their own.

How does Ofsted respond to 'thinking' geography departments? There is a risk that Ofsted's view of school improvement and school self evaluation debate might be based on a narrow focus of purely raising standards in terms of GCSE or equivalent qualifications: gap closing rather than planning for longer term improvement eg, targeting C/D boundary rather than addressing underlying structural problems such as the poor use of prior achievement data and/or careful monitoring of pupil progress and intervention programmes. In short, there needs to be more guidance and training for inspectors to provide them with the necessary understanding of thinking skills and their development and use in the classroom.

Can the value of developing thinking skills only be judged in terms of improvements achieved in assessment results?

Are the present examinations able to provide an appropriate and challenging mechanism for assessing the capabilities of students who have developed their thinking skills to a high Level?

Do the pupils' perceptions about the geographical education they receive match the teacher and departmental learning objectives?

Will young people actually recognise the potential and value of acquiring thinking skills in geography, or indeed in any curricular area? Research into pupils' perceptions about the geographical education they receive can highlight some worrying mismatches when compared to teacher and departmental objectives. When asked 'How do you think geography prepares you for life in the 21st Century', one group of Key Stage 3 pupils' responses were as shown in *Figure 10.5*.

It is important to explicitly share learning objectives, and in particular to engage pupils in metacognition, so that they are able to recognise and appreciate the role of geographical education in their futures.

Figure 10.2 **A DEPARTMENTAL VISION FOR GEOGRAPHICAL EDUCATION**

PLANNING FOR LEARNING

Focus on long, medium and short term planning for learning (in addition to planning for teaching content). To include:

Explicit sharing of learning objectives with pupils

Thinking skills - including progression

Explicit teaching of key geographical concepts

Mental models

Cognitive skills

Whole brain learning

Metacognition

Construction and social construction

Transfer

Big picture - process and content

Modelling

Reciprocity

Scaffolding

Reflection

Debriefing

Moving away from models designed to control learners

Learning environment

Displays in all geography classrooms that support learning initiatives eg, literacy support via non fiction writing genre starters and connectives, geographical enquiry framework, mind maps to illustrate the big picture for all units of study.

Assessment

Increase number of Key Stage 3 assessment activities with *TTG* stimulus.

Link examination command words to non fiction writing genre.

Use of classroom display in supporting recall eg, big picture, key concepts.

Developing education for **values and attitudes**

NC for geography - especially global citizenship,

environmental change and sustainable development.

NC for citizenship.

PSHE including SMSC.

Post-modern thinking

Making sense of a world full of uncertainties, multiple and partial truths.

Outcomes for department

More focused annual development planning.

Greater collaboration - team spirit.

Shared good practice, within department and beyond - heightened profile of geography.

Improved assessment outcomes.

Higher order thinking skills - develop beyond the use of 'off the peg' activities.

Establish teacher understanding of how 'thinking strategies' support various types of learning eg, recall, understanding of processes and concepts, literacy skills, geographical skills etc.

Investigate their use as literacy interventions - text, sentence, word level.

Develop activities that deliver aspects of citizenship education.

Carry out classroom research into reductions in pupil disaffection and incidences of indiscipline.

Develop use of alternative texts (words, images, sounds… from a range of sources).

Develop critical literacy of those texts.

Embrace elements of the **National Literacy Strategy**

Writing interventions to support and develop non fiction writing genre.

Reading interventions.

Outcomes for teachers

Improved teacher confidence and self esteem.

Broader repertoire of teaching strategies.

Understanding of how children learn.

Fewer discipline issues - less stress.

Outcomes for the learners of all abilities and social background

Greater enjoyment of learning.

Fewer discipline problems.

Greater pupil motivation inside and beyond the classroom.

Improved achievement and attainment.

Young people who do 'give a damn'.

Figure 10.3 GEOGRAPHY DEPARTMENT ANNUAL DEVELOPMENT PLAN (extract)

S.D.P. CODE	SCHOOL DEVELOPMENT PLAN KEY ISSUE	LEADERSHIP	SUCCESS CRITERIA	TARGETS	INDIVIDUAL TEACHER TRAINING NEEDS	DEPARTMENT TRAINING NEEDS	EVALUATION DATE
A7	FOCUS ON SHORT, MEDIUM AND LONG TERM PLANNING FOR IMPROVED LEARNING INCLUDING THE DEVELOPMENT OF THINKING AND LITERACY SKILLS	LT	Learning strategy column completed and evaluated for 2 units of study in each of years 7, 8 and 9 - to show evidence of more explicit planning of learning strategies that support and develop recall, understanding and skills, reading and writing skills, values and attitudes.	**Insertion of 'Learning Strategy' column in KS3 schemes of work** To clarify and focus understanding of what is to be learned and approaches to achieving this - incorporation into existing and newly introduced Y7 units of study from QCA - *'Making Connections'* and *'Flood Disaster - How do People Cope?'* Also more varied learning strategies across KS3, incorporating multi-sensory approaches.	LT to attend *Accelerated Learning* course, Manchester November. LT to consider published research into learning.	LT to lead department session on whole school training day and at 6 half termly departmental meetings (half agenda to be devoted to introducing 6 units of study).	March
	RESPOND TO RESEARCH INTO THE HUMAN BRAIN AND LEARNING	LT	Each member of the department to have employed selected strategies and fed back at evaluation session.	More opportunities for **oral work** - especially the development of **reciprocity.**		SD to lead dept. meeting on 'circle time' and other strategies, October.	November
		LT/SDG	LT, DAA, CMC, NMH, SDG and RJH to have participated in classroom research project. SDG to have produced ICT based support hyperlinking enquiry components to writing frames. LT to have recorded and presented research to SMT and at LEA literacy meeting February.	Use of **modelling** and **scaffolding** via **literacy** focused activities incorporating ICT.	LT and SDG to receive training from literacy coordinator. SDG to train in using hyperlinks. LT to participate in LEA literacy pilot for KS3.	Literacy coordinator to lead departmental meeting and launch classroom research project, November. LT to lead evaluation of research, March.	March
		LT	Mind map posters generated for all GCSE units - on classroom walls.	Use of **big picture** as a learning framework.	See *Accelerated Learning* course above.	LT to lead dept. meeting, December.	March
		LT/CMC	Professional Development Review proforma produced and trialled in LT's and CMC's lessons.	Development of pupil **metacognition** via planned and structured **debriefing.**	LT to consider Leat's *TTG* book and research project.	LT to lead development of departmental 'lesson observation' proforma for use in professional development review cycle annually.	March
		LT	Outcomes fed back to department at dept. meeting. To include learning resources, pupil logs, teacher journal (video in some cases).	Each member of department to 'develop' an agreed aspect of their teaching using research evidence.	LT to work with individuals in planning.	Outcomes shared with all members of the department via meetings.	March

Figure 10.4 LESSON OBSERVATION PROFORMA				
Learning Focus	**M**	**I**	**C**	**Comment**
Explicit sharing of learning objectives with pupils				
Connecting with prior learning (construction)				
Explicit sharing of the 'big picture' - process and content				
Explicit teaching of key geographical concepts				
Acknowledgement of challenge and the 'zone of proximal development'				
Thinking skills activities				
Use of mental models				
Opportunities for whole brain learning (logic and gestalt)				
Cycles of 'focus' and 'diffuse'				
Development of metacognition				
Transfer of learning within geography and to other curricular areas				
Modelling of learning				
Developing reciprocity				
Scaffolding of learning activities				
Learning activated via multiple intelligences				
- visual				
- auditory				
- kinaesthetic				
- other				
Opportunities for reflection and review				
Planned debriefing activity				

M = Maintain   I = Improve   C = Change   to be negotiated prior to the lesson observation in order to establish appropriate foci

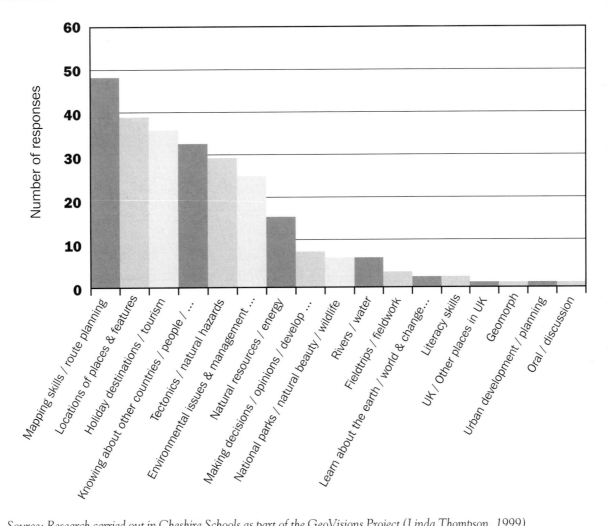

Figure 10.5 **HOW DOES GEOGRAPHY PREPARE YOU FOR LIFE IN THE 21st CENTURY?**

Source: Research carried out in Cheshire Schools as part of the GeoVisions Project (Linda Thompson, 1999)

　　　　　　More Thinking Through Geography

Chapter 11

Infusing Geography Schemes of Work with Teaching Thinking

11 Infusing Geography Schemes of Work with Teaching Thinking

Perhaps the most important principle in devising a scheme of work which does more than just dip into Thinking Skills is to aim to teach beyond a narrow conception of the facts and skills needed for either progression through NC Levels or examination success ie, above Level 2 use (see *Introduction*). *TTG* is about having high expectations and helping pupils acquire the *means* to be successful learners by becoming better thinkers. As with other geographical skills, pupils can become better thinkers with instruction and practice. Our job as teachers is to plan for progression in cognitive skills when putting schemes of work and lessons together, and to ensure that this is both explicit and accessible for department members and pupils. If we do, the chances of pupils really understanding their geography, and of taking their learning beyond the lesson or examination will be enhanced.

Thinking Skills lessons often appeal to a wider range of senses than do didactic or traditional resource based teaching. When planning we should therefore be conscious of the variety of ways in which children learn. A useful model is Howard Gardner's 'frames of mind' or 'multiple intelligences' (Gardner, 1983) and discussed in Fisher, (1990). British education has traditionally put a high premium on *logical/mathematical intelligence*. It is well represented in *TTG* strategies and can be closely related to NCTS Reasoning Skills. It is the ability to churn problems in one's head and reach logical conclusions. Some pupils will respond well to the use of spoken or written language and be able to communicate their understanding in the same ways *(verbal-linguistic intelligence)*. Others will learn better through pictures and be able to form complex visual images in their mind's eye *(visual-spatial intelligence)*. Similarly some children relish the opportunity to debate and share ideas *(interpersonal intelligence)*, while others prefer to internalise new ideas, make connections and reach their own conclusions *(intrapersonal intelligence)*. Through the use of well sequenced Teaching Thinking strategies we can allow all pupils to work in their preferred 'frames of mind' at **some time**, while giving them scope for improving their learning capacity in others. For example, **Predicting with Video** works well for those with visual/spatial and verbal/linguistic aptitudes, as does **Concept Maps** which also plays to the strengths of interpersonal learners and of course, the logical thinkers.

Teaching Thinking also gives a high profile to Big Concepts that are fundamental to understanding the subject *(See Introduction)*. Lessons and other learning activities should be planned to progressively and coherently develop pupils' conceptual framework or understanding of the 'big picture'.

Part of the planning process should address the way in which these are introduced, developed and transferred, so that pupils begin to see geographical patterns and connections. For example you may be aiming to develop an understanding of decision making to enhance examination success at GCSE. Rather than ploughing straight into exam style decision making exercises, it might be helpful to incorporate strategies such as **5W**, **Making Animals** and **Layered Decision Making** to practise and discuss generic skills to make elements of the decision making process more visible and explicit.

One of the aims of Thinking Skills activities, especially through debriefing, is to introduce pupils to the language of thinking. This enables them to discuss their approaches to tasks. However, language can be a barrier to learning when it is used inappropriately. It helps if pupils feel they have ownership of the words and phrases they need, whether these are subject specific terms or the vocabulary that describes their cognitive processes. It is important to introduce and use 'thinking words' as part of the activity or debrief in a structured way. An example helps here: pupils are unlikely to be able to understand the principle of *justifying* their responses if they are unfamiliar with the concept of *evidence*, therefore the latter term needs to be used first. A **Mystery** (see *TTG*) can be used to *identify* and *describe* evidence, before a solution is *evaluated*. Pupils can be provided with definitions of relevant thinking words that may help understand and explain their cognitive processes. (See *Appendix*) They could, for example, be asked to organise these words into the order in which they think they did each one: read, discuss, understand, sort, rank, link, analyse, explain. As they become familiar with the terminology, its range can be expanded.

Through the introduction of the National Literacy Strategy we should be encountering a generation of pupils who are used to manipulating language at word, sentence and text level. The whole-class plenary sessions during which they present, review and consolidate their learning is mirrored in the *TTG* debriefing phase. Long term planning can consider how TT can be used to build on these foundations of literacy.

Another issue to be addressed is the need for assessment of, and improvement in, pupil performance. The NC Level descriptions can seem blunt and cumbersome, and are not very helpful in supporting pupil progress through formative assessment. Debriefing is important in providing instant feedback (see *Debriefing*) but other opportunities for assessment for learning need to be coherently planned into schemes of work. Black and Dockrell's useful model (1980) differentiates between modular, longitudinal and background intended outcomes:

TYPE OF INTENDED OUTCOME AND EXPLANATION	GEOGRAPHICAL EXAMPLE
Background Fundamental to the subject and learning experience, but not always made explicit to the pupils or really assessed.	We have altered physical systems to both good and bad effect.
Longitudinal Common features relating to the learning of the subject across a number of units, often skills and ideas that are taught or rehearsed intermittently.	Decision making involves evaluating evidence and solving conflicts.
Modular Specific to a section of work, often the most immediately obvious to pupils.	Low pressure weather systems bring wet and windy conditions.

It is easy for one's attention to focus on the immediacy of the modular outcomes in our assessment and less attention to be paid to process skills and the Big Concepts that *TTG* strategies promote.

So what does all this mean in the reality of planning schemes of work? It is unlikely that all of the above issues can be addressed immediately or within a single unit of work, so try a range of approaches. For example:

- Use 3 **Mysteries** and 3 **Making Animals** in Y7 making the demands progressively more challenging;

- Choose a concept such as *cause and effect* or decision making and plan how this will be explored during one year;

- Choose an important co-operative skill, such as listening to others' opinions, and ask pupils to reflect in their planner or exercise book how their understanding of its importance and their ability in it are developing;

- Select three activities involving, say, 'prioritisation', and consider carefully how to introduce this term meaningfully to pupils.

The best schemes of work will not come 'off the shelf', but will be developed by individuals working co-operatively within departments and between schools. They will be grounded in a sound knowledge of their own pupils' strengths and weaknesses, and involve a good deal of creative thinking at the planning and evaluation stages. They will be flexible and adaptable in response to successes and failures with teachers and their pupils.

Below is a scheme of work designed for the Urban Issues unit of Edexcel GCSE Syllabus B edited down to only where *TTG* strategies are employed and to illustrate that they are capable of delivering 'content' and teaching thinking at the same time. Except where it takes up the bulk of the lesson, the *TTG* strategy is embedded within more 'conventional' tasks and activities, including, yes, using text books. They make for a stimulating range of 40 minute lessons, catering for the movers, lookers, talkers, readers, organisers, drawers and problem solvers.

The principle aims of this unit are that pupils should:

1 Systematically develop their thinking processes and skills through the lessons and homework.

2 Gain access to the curriculum through the use of activities drawing on a range of 'intelligences' to cater for the wide range of learning styles.

3 Gain knowledge and understanding of the topic.

SCHEME OF WORK: URBAN ISSUES, Edexcel GCSE Syllabus 3		
Lesson	**Content / issues**	**Thinking Skills Strategy**
1	Growing demand for new homes in UK. Although UK population is not growing rapidly, many more new homes are required at the turn of 21st Century. Consider causes eg, more single households, old properties, counter-urbanisation. Introduce idea that demand is not uniform.	**Mystery** (TTG) 'Why couldn't Billy Davies afford the new home he wanted?'
2	Housing development on brownfield and greenfield sites. Define terms. Use photos / estate agent details / local news cuttings / students' experience / planning proposals. Consider pros and cons of each in local environment.	**Most Likely To....** Brownfield / greenfield sites.
3	Greenfield sites and the rural urban fringe. Why people have opposing views regarding greenfield housing. Include quality of life and hidden cost.	**Layered Decision Making**
4	Brownfield sites. OS maps / aerial photos / photos of urban brownfield site(s). Timeline for use of site eg, industrial growth, decline, dereliction, redevelopment.	**5W** Exercise to establish problems and potential for housing use.
5	Urbanisation in LEDCs. Statistics / atlas work. Define push and pull factors, and brainstorm examples.	**Living Graphs** (TTG) **Odd One Out** (TTG) Push / pull factors.
6	Case study Jakarta. Push and pull factors for rural Indonesia / Jakarta. Population pyramid / age profile for city, linking to high rates of natural increase.	**Concept Maps**
7	Life in Jakarta. Profiles of residents to consider housing, environmental and employment conditions. Cartoon strip / speech bubbles to write up conversations between residents.	**Storytelling** (TTG) **Mind Movies** (TTG)
8	'Build your own home' game. Shanty town self help scheme.	**Making Animals** Making Houses.
9	Problems of urban traffic.	**Odd One Out** Traffic (TTG). To introduce issues and determine level of understanding.
10	Traffic management case study.	**Classification** Role of individuals, authorities, business etc (TTG).

Chapter 12

Debriefing

12 Debriefing

One of the most common comments we hear is that the Teaching Thinking activities work and really challenge the students but that the talking / discussion bit at the end is frequently allowed to slip by undone. The *Introduction* to both this and the first *TTG* book identified **debriefing** as the chief characteristic of the third of the four levels at which *TTG* strategies can be implemented. The key principle underpinning *TTG* is that pupils become better thinkers and therefore learners if they think and understand more about the thinking processes. This is **metacognition**. This adds value to their learning by promoting the transfer of thinking across subjects and situations; in other words, helping students become autonomous learners.

'Thinking' as a buzz word is proliferating in geography education literature, including some textbooks where its appropriateness is debatable. I would argue that teaching thinking necessitates debriefing. Otherwise, good geography teaching it might be, but teaching thinking…? The Teaching Thinking model (*Figure 11.1*) shows where debriefing fits into the process.

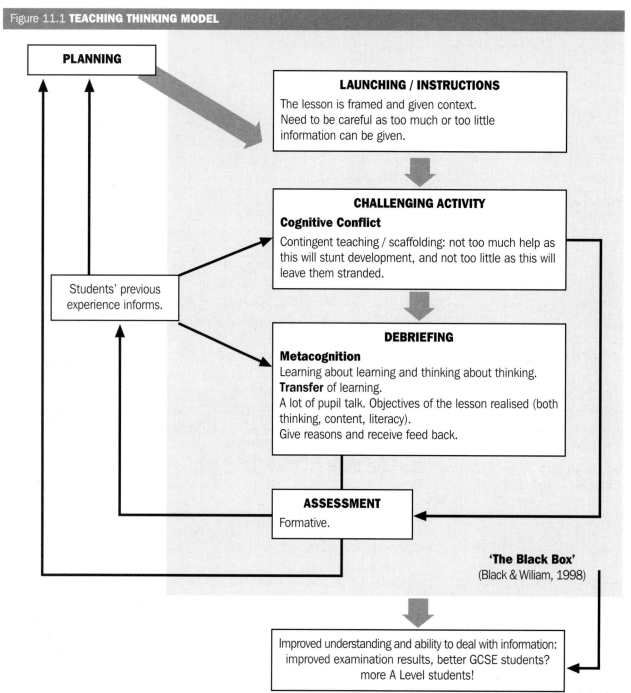

Figure 11.1 **TEACHING THINKING MODEL**

More Thinking Through Geography

Debriefing is the plenary phase at the end of the lesson usually involving the whole class setting, though sometimes less formal debriefing occurs within groups. The teacher plays an important role in connecting the new thinking to other contexts in order to generalise the learning and help create models that the students can use to transfer their learning to other contexts.

Much of the research that forms the basis of this section comes from a TTA sponsored research project: *'Debriefing: Pupils' Learning and Teacher Planning'* carried out by members of the *TTG* group. It involved video recording, debriefing the lesson and interviews with students based on two questions: *'What did you learn during the lesson?'* and *'What did the teacher do to help you learn?'*

What are the typical characteristics of a debriefed lesson?

The two main characteristics of a debriefed lesson are the large number of open questions asked and the extended answers that pupils give. The questions that the teachers ask contain an element of risk as the teacher does not have a specific answer in mind. The questions are difficult and require thought before being answered. Thinking time and extended responses are not major features of traditional classrooms where the average response time for students to answer is around two seconds and response length much the same. In debriefed lessons student answers are often over half a minute in length. There are often pauses in these answers and pupils are encouraged to 'go on'.

In debriefed lessons teachers also make frequent reference to the Big Concepts and more generic skills such as listening, describing, comparing and literacy. Pupils are comfortable with discussing these and many references are made to other learning contexts with which students are familiar. These are often exemplified by the teacher using analogies or stories to help with the transfer.

Teachers provide criteria by which pupils can judge their thinking and its outcomes.

What do pupils learn from debriefed lessons?

There are four main strands to what pupils learn from debriefed lessons. The first is **geography.** It is a false assumption that the National Curriculum or GCSE syllabus does not allow time or scope for TT. We would contest that students learn geography more effectively through it, as the CASE and CAME projects have successfully demonstrated in science and maths. We would not advocate it otherwise.

Debriefing often focuses on **learning skills.** Pupils develop their ability to handle and process information and reach conclusions to challenging tasks collaboratively. The *TTG* philosophy encourages group activity: learning is a social process so TT develops **social skills.** Pupils are quite willing to listen to their peers and to make constructive comment about what they heard and how they learned from and through each other. They value the experience, as the extract from the post lesson interview extract shows.

The last strand is that of **wider learning**, and the recognition that skills and ideas are transferable to other curriculum contexts and beyond. Learning is not *just* for examinations, much of which is 'surface learning'; it is deep learning; lifelong learning.

What is the teacher's role in the debriefing process?

There are a number of roles for the teacher to play in the debriefing process. One of the most important of these is to **promote and manage discussion.** Pupils value this discussion if they can see the benefit of it. It is up to the teacher to help this to happen in both small groups and in whole class debriefing episodes. The teacher also needs to be careful that he or she does not give too much away or interrupt groups at work. You are there to facilitate. The teacher has a major role in the whole class debriefing to **collate ideas** or strategies that pupils have used in tackling tasks so that these can be considered and evaluated by the whole class. This allows the good thinking to be shared.

One of the major characteristics of debriefing episodes is the extent to which it immediately **provides feedback** to individuals. This formative assessment is extremely important to students and there is substantial research evidence that this can significantly raise achievement. It is not just the teacher who should be providing the feedback but they should also be encouraging the students to do so to their peers. It is important that all pupil

It is made clear in the introduction that lessons and debriefing need a rationale.

Exemplar 1 of **Taboo** and *Exemplar 1 and 2* of **5W** highlight some standard debriefing open questions.

The matrix at the end of the *Introduction* shows how the Big Concepts are addressed in the Exemplars.

Exemplar 1 of **Concept Maps** illustrates how good geography was learned and highlighted through debriefing.

Taboo and *Exemplar 3* of **5W** highlights how debriefing can help develop literacy skills.

Maps From Memory is an activity that highlights the benefits of and can develop good social and groupwork skills.

Working with Others is a Key Skill in the NC.

This is important in facilitating transfer of learning.

If assessment is to be 'for learning', then debriefing is the key.

reasoning is valued (this does not mean that it cannot be criticised) as this provides them with confidence and improved self-esteem.

In debriefing episodes pupils are often asked to **explain their thinking** in detail. Much of this explanation is lengthy and in contrast to what is seen in many classrooms. The teacher can facilitate this by not interrupting, in fact by waiting or asking for them to 'say a bit more' or to 'go on'.

Exemplar 1 of **Making Animals** illustrates how good connections can be made using anologies.

Good debriefing in TT lessons will encourage students to **make connections** between existing and new learning and will **provide heuristics** (a general problem solving strategy). When teachers help pupils to make connections they are providing the foundation of transfer of learning; this can often be aided by the use of an analogy or a story. An example of an analogy used in a **Fact or Opinion** (*TTG*) exercise was 'the Spice Girls are rubbish' and 'Newcastle United is the best team in Europe'. These provoked a lot of discussion, which was eventually serious! Many of the strategies (such as **5W** and **Concept Maps**) are generic in that they can be used in many curricular contexts by students once their use is understood. Some may begin to do so independently but the teacher's role in supporting understanding of the use of these strategies is most important for the vast majority. Simply using a strategy without debriefing misses part of its value.

Tips for successful debriefing

- Start with a short debrief of a relatively straightforward (although challenging) activity such as **Taboo**. Plan the debriefing focus and identify the appropriate questions to pose. Begin by asking them how they went about the task. Be aware of the TT vocabulary that is likely to be involved and that you may need to introduce to help build a language of thinking. (see *Appendix*)

- Use the Planning for Debriefing proforma (*Figure 11.2*) to help you formulate some of the ideas that you will be exploring and the ways in which you will explore them. Eventually your use of this sheet will dwindle until you do not need it. You will then be a debriefing expert.

- Be prepared to allow students to talk at length and encourage them to do so by saying 'and..' or 'go on..' or suggesting that they go on with a hand gesture.

- Give the pupils time to think about their answers, do not be afraid of silence, or chat, while they are doing this. You could perhaps even formalise this by saying *'I'll give you a minute to discuss this'* before asking for a group to feedback.

- Use groups because pupils will support and encourage each other in their discussion and thinking.

- Make sure students see the point of the lesson. Feel free to summarise or round up the lesson yourself.

- Get the students to evaluate each other's answer. How could it be improved upon?

- But don't over plan, as this can be too restricting for both you and the pupils. Think about transfer contexts, but not to the point where you will give them – ask the pupils.

- Don't interrupt a pupil when you have got the answer you are wanting. In fact don't have too many preconceived notions about what the answer should look like.

- Pay attention to what groups are doing during the activity, even write down some things, as this will give you some good starting points during the debriefing. It will allow you to say *'this group did something quite interesting, why don't you tell us about it'*.

- Don't just settle for a one word answer: ask pupils to explain their reasoning. Don't take over the answer.

- Make your lessons stimulating and make sure the tasks are challenging, otherwise there is little to debrief.

- If it doesn't work first time *don't give it up*. It will take both you and your classes time to get used to it and it is worthwhile. *Appendix 1* may help here. Don't be afraid of having risk and ambiguity in your classroom.

- Above all, *plan* for debriefing time.

These following exchanges exemplify how debriefing helps pupils to recognise their own
and their peers' roles in the learning process – steps towards becoming autonomous learners.

Visiting teacher interviewing pupils after debriefing session (edited)

Teacher (T): So we've got to the stage where we're thinking about the lesson. We've
got the bits and envelopes; you've sorted the things into piles. You've agreed in your
group finally after a bit of discussion ... OK, do you think the discussion is a good thing?

Girl (G)1: Yeah ... because you get other peoples' ideas as well as your own.

T: Craig had a go at comparing and what did Mr K say about his
go at comparing?

G2: He asked us if that was comparing?

B: I didn't think it was. I thought it was wrong.

T: So what was Mr K doing then?

G: Trying to get us to answer ... to add points to it.

B: The next time we do it – what things to do, what things not to do.

(later)

B: I... just thought it was a normal lesson.

T: A normal lesson and you didn't think that he had this cunning plan?

B: He covered a lot of stuff. He talks about stuff ... he tells you what
you're doing. If you get mixed up he tells you how others are doing it.

G2: He'll try and get a lot of people involved.

T: Do you like that?

Chorus: Yeah!

T: You don't mind your friends correcting you?

G2: No. I'm not bothered ... If they don't, you just do it wrong the
next time.

Groupwork and whole
class discussion facilitates
sharing of good ideas and
practice.

Students appreciate the
immediate formative
feedback that they get in
debriefing episodes.

Figure 11.2: **PLANNING FOR DEBRIEFING**

Classroom activity: (including content)	**Concepts or skills focused on:**		**Date:**	**Time:**
			Class Information:	

Focus:

Whole group/small group/pairs/individual

Debriefing objectives:

For pupils

For self

Briefing:

Key features of task/launching

Analogies/examples to be used:

Pupils' comments overheard:

Used:

Context:

Previous attempts

Class-related factors

Debriefing:

Debriefing questions:

Outcome = O

Interpersonal = I

Mental = M

Transfer context to be suggested:

Key words/terms/vocabulary:

Follow-up tasks/homework:

Appendix

A Glossary of Thinking Skills

TTG activities may be approached and integrated into one's teaching in a variety of ways but it is at and above Level 3 (see *Introduction*) that debriefing helps both teacher and pupil develop a consciousness about ways of thinking. We have mentioned at a number points in both *TTG* books that discussing cognitive processes rarely occurs naturally. In addition to trying to deconstruct abstract processes we need an appropriate vocabulary with which to articulate our ideas. (Have you ever tried discussing the pattern of play in a game of American football with an American?)

One could argue that all voluntary activity (physical or intellectual) requires thought. We are thinking all the time. But we can help pupils and ourselves to develop a vocabulary for the *kinds* of thinking we are engaged in. We hesitate to include what follows lest someone complains that they have to learn the terms before getting involved. Not so. It is simply intended to help teachers and pupils identify, understand and codify their thinking processes of both high and low order.

Thinking is a process, so the terms below are all verbs describing what you do intellectually. The definitions alongside are interpretations of dictionary definitions to suit the educational context. From a professional developmental perspective, it is well worth examining a selection of recent lessons (perhaps across the department) for different year groups. Examine them from the perspective of 'cognitive challenge' and progression. Lack of it lies at the heart of what Ofsted sometimes refers to as 'low expectations of pupils'. Pupils make real progress when they achieve something that is *more* challenging than what they did before so we need to be aware of what that entails and to respond to it in our planning. This glossary, which is by no means exhaustive, has been phrased, we hope, in a friendly way.

Thinking Skill To....	Definition Means....
adapt	to adjust to
adopt	to choose to accept
amalgamate	to combine or blend into one
apply	to put to a relevant use
assess	to evaluate or estimate the value of
characterise	to describe using the distinctive features of
combine	to join together or unite
compare	to look for similarities
compromise	to reach agreement by each side making concessions
contrast	to look for differences
convert	to change the form of
decide	to reach a decision, to settle an issue in your mind
decipher	to discover the meaning of something perhaps written in a code
decode	to find the meaning of something in a code
deconstruct	to analyse by dismantling to expose how something works
define	to describe something by its qualities and circumstances
develop	to evolve from a simple to a more advanced state
differentiate	to make different
discriminate	to recognise differences between
distinguish	to tell apart
employ	to use or set to work
evaluate	to judge the value of
examine	to investigate, to consider critically, to weigh and sift arguments
explain	to say why

Thinking Skill To....	Definition Means....
extrapolate	to project from given data
forecast	to predict, foresee or calculate beforehand
formulate	to set out in a methodical way
generalise	to widely apply statements based on a number of case studies
hypothesise	to float an idea or propose a limited explanation as a basis for investigation
identify	to recognise something by analysis
imagine	to suppose, to form an idea or image in the mind
implement	to put into effect
interpolate	to insert into a series
interpret	to explain the meaning of
interrelate	to find the connections between two or more things
judge	to examine evidence and form an opinion to hear a case and reach a verdict
juxtapose	to place one thing alongside another
manipulate	to move things about with skill
model	to create a description that exemplifies how something happens
negotiate	to discuss in order to reach a deal or agreement
order	to methodically arrange things
organise	to arrange parts into a 'living whole'
paraphrase	to restate in a new way to make something clearer
plan	make preparations for
predict	say what will happen in the future
present	to show or offer for consideration
prioritize	to organise tasks in order of importance
rank	to arrange things in order of importance
recall	to remember
recognise	to recall the identity of something or somebody
reconstruct	to rebuild or reassemble
reflect	to think deeply about past events, actions or thoughts
reorganise	to arrange parts differently into a 'living whole'
restructure	to create a new framework for to put together again in a different way
reword	to put into other words
scan	to examine closely to identify information
skim	to look at something quickly to identify the main points
structure	to create a framework for to put together
summarise	to make a brief version of something
synthesise	to combine into a complex whole
test	to verify by experiment
transfer	to move something from one location or context to another
transform	to change the way in which something is presented
translate	to interpret or express in clearer terms
validate	to verify or confirm
visualise	to see in your mind's eye

(After Ralph Hare, 9.12.00)

Bibliography

Bennett, N.
(1995) Managing learning through group work, in Desforges, C. (Ed.),
An Introduction to Teaching: Psychological Perspectives,
Oxford: Blackwell

Bigge, M.L. & Shermis, S.S.
(1998) *Learning Theories for Teachers*,
Harlow: Longman

Black, H.D. & Dockrell, W.B.
(1980) *Diagnostic Assessment in Secondary Schools*
Sevenoaks: Hodder & Stoughton

Black, P. & Wiliam, D.
(1998) 'Assessment and Classroom Learning', in
Assessment in Education, 5,1.

Butt, G.
(1991) Have We Got a Video Today?
in Teaching Geography *Vol. 16 (2)*

Chapman, N.
(2000) Unpublished M.Ed. dissertation,
Does Thinking Through Geography Add Value to Geography GCSE Pupils?
University of Newcastle

Cook, F., Harris, H., Lofthouse, & Rockett, M.
(1997) *GCSE Geography*
Ormskirk: Causeway Press

Davidson, G. & Catling, S.
(2000) Ch.19 in Chris Fisher & Tony Binns, *Issues in Geography*,
London: Routledge: Falmer

de Bono, E.
(1992) *Teach Your Child How To Think*
London: Viking

DfEE
(1999) *The National Literacy Strategy Key Stage 3 Literacy Conference Manual*
London: DfEE

DfEE
(1999) *The National Curriculum Handbook for Secondary Teachers in England,
Key Stages 1–3*
London: DfEE

DfEE
(2000) *The Hay McBer Report: A Model of Teacher Effectiveness.*
London: DfEE

Dillon, J. T.
(1988) *Questioning and Teaching: A Manual of Practice.*
London: Croom Helm

Erickson, H. L.
(1998) *Concept-Based Curriculum and Instruction.*
London: Corwin Press

Fisher, R.
(1990) *Teaching Children to Think.* Ch.1
Oxford: Blackwell

Fisher, C. & Binns, A.
(2000) *Issues in Geography Teaching.*
London: Routledge: Falmer

Gardner, H.
(1983) *Frames of Mind: The Theory of Multiple Intelligences.*
New York: Basic Books

Ghaye, A. & Robinson, E.
(1989) Concept Maps and Children's Thinking: a Constructivist Approach in Slater, F.
(Ed) *Language and Learning in the Teaching of Geography*
London: Routledge

Guiness, P. & Nagel, G.
(1999) *AS Geography: Concepts and Cases*
London: Hodder Educational

Hopkin, J. (2000) *Geography Matters 1 Higher*
Oxford: Heinemann

King, S.
(1999) Using Questions to Promote Learning
in *Teaching Geography Vol. 24 (4)*

Leat, D. (Ed)
(1998) *Thinking Through Geography*
Cambridge: Chris Kington Publishing

Leat, D. & Chandler, S.
(1996) Using Concept Mapping in Geography Teaching
in *Teaching Geography Vol. 23(3)*

Leat, D. & Kinninment, D.
(2000) Ch.11 in Chris Fisher & Tony Binns, *Issues in Geography*,
London: Routledge: Falmer

Leat, D. & McAleavy. T.
(1998) Critical Thinking in the Humanities in *Teaching Geography, Vol. 23 (3)*

Leat, D. & Nichols, A.
(1999) *Mysteries Make You Think*
Sheffield: Geographical Association

McGuinness, C.
(1999) *From Thinking Skills to Thinking Classrooms*,
Research Report No.115
London: DfEE

Olsen & Gee
(1991) in Wray, D. & Lewis, M. (1997) *Extending Literacy*
London: Routledge

QCA
(2000) *Geography - A Scheme of Work for Key Stage 3,*
London: QCA/DfEE

Roberts, M.
(1987), Using Videocassettes
in *Teaching Geography, Vol. 12 (3)*

SCAA
(1996) *Geography Optional Tests and Tasks, Unit 2: Earthquakes*
London: SCAA

Waugh, D.
(1994) *The Wider World*,
Walton on Thames: Nelson

Waugh, D. & Bushell, T.
(1993) *Key Geography: Interactions*
Cheltenham: Stanley Thornes

Wray, D. & Lewis, M.
(1997) *Extending Literacy*
London: Routledge
www.dfee.gov.uk/teachingreforms/mcber/oz.htm

Further useful reading:

Adey, P. & Shayer, M.
(1993) *Really Raising Standards*
London: Routledge

Hart, S.
(2000) *Thinking Through Teaching*
London: David Fulton Publishers

Hughes, M.
(1999) *Closing the Gap*
Stafford: Network Education Press

Jordan, R.R. & Powell,S.D.
(1991) Teaching Thinking: The Case for Principles
in *European Journal of Special Needs, Vol. 6 (2)*

Lipman, M.
(1991) *Thinking in Education*
Cambridge: Cambridge University Press

Perkins, D.
(1992) *Smart School: Better Thinking and Learning for Every Child*
New York: Free Press

Quinn, V.
(1997) *Critical Thinking in Young Minds*
London: David Fulton Publishers

Smith, A.
(1998) *Accelerated Learning*
Stafford: Network Educational Press

White, R. & Gunstone, R.
(1992) *Probing Understanding*
London: Falmer Press

Wood, D.
(1988) *How Children Think and Learn*
Oxford: Blackwell